D1382560

HoW TO
SPEaK
CaT

A GUIDE TO DECODING
CAT LANGUAGE

Aline Alexander Newman
& Gary Weitzman, D.V.M.

President & CEO of the
San Diego Humane Society and SPCA

NATIONAL
GEOGRAPHIC

WASHINGTON, D.C.

CoNTENTS

Burmese

MEET DR. GARY

VETERINARIAN AND CAT EXPERT

A CAT CAN BE your very best friend. It can be your muse, your protector, your little hunter, or your guide. Cats can be predictable, mysterious, or just plain crazy! But to get the most out of your relationship, you need to be able to communicate. Our furry felines already speak at least a little "human". Now it's time for us to catch up to them and learn to speak "cat".

My name is Dr. Gary Weitzman, and I'm going to be your guide throughout this book. I've been a veterinarian and animal rescuer for more than 20 years. I'm currently the president of the San Diego Humane Society and SPCA in California, U.S.A. I spend a lot of time making sure animals are well cared for, have homes, and receive medical care and attention. Taking care of animals goes a whole lot further when you understand what they need. Learning to read their body language, see into their eyes, and listen to their sounds can tell you exactly what they're saying. And, in some cases, it can even save lives.

I've known many cats throughout my career. In fact, at the Humane Society, we have a kitten nursery dedicated to saving the lives of orphaned kittens from all over San Diego. Last year, we saved more than 1,500 kittens in one summer alone. I hope every single one of them is teaching their new families how to speak and understand cat fluently!

Throughout this book, I'll let you in on different tips and strategies for communicating effectively and accurately with your cat, your neighbour's cat, or a stray that comes up to your door wanting food or shelter or company. You'll learn where cats come from, how to read cat body language, and so much more. Most important, you'll also learn how to help cats read you. Cats are complex. But once we know what to expect from them and how to understand what they're "saying", a lot of the mystery goes away. Today, scientists are learning so much more about how animals think. Animals are more like us than we ever thought. So we shouldn't be surprised to learn that cats, often our closest companions, are trying to talk to us every single day, using their voices, eyes, ears, and even tails. They understand us so much better than we understand them. It's time to set the record straight—all animals communicate, with each other, with their young, with predators and their prey, and with us. In the nearly 3,500 years since the first cats came to live with humans in ancient Egypt, they've learned how to communicate with us. It's time for us to learn how to talk back.

So keep reading to learn about the wonderful language of cats. They'll be grateful that you know how to speak to them, as well as they have learned how to speak to us!

Unless otherwise labelled, the cats pictured throughout this book are American (or domestic) shorthairs with various colour patterns, such as tabby or calico.

FOR YOUR SAFETY

While National Geographic has worked to make sure the following training tips, scenarios, and interpretations of cat behaviour come from the most accurate and up-to-date sources, you should know that cats, like all animals, can be unpredictable.

No matter how careful you are, no matter how many rules you follow, things can go wrong. Also, much of the advice and guidance in this book requires close observation of cats; there may be nuances of behaviour that the observer can miss. So even though this book is packed with advice from the experts, there is no guarantee that such advice will work in any specific situation. Always be cautious with cats that are strangers to you and careful with cats with whom you are familiar.

All content and information published in this book is provided to the reader "as is" and without any guarantees. The situations and activities described carry inherent risks and hazards. The reader must evaluate and accept all risks associated with the use of the information provided in this book, including those risks associated with reliance on the accuracy, thoroughness, utility, or appropriateness of the information for any particular situation. The authors and publisher specifically disclaim all responsibility for any liability, loss, or risk, personal or otherwise, that is incurred as a consequence of the application of any of the contents in this book.

WHAT IS A CaT?

COAT: The colour, length, texture, and thickness of a cat's coat varies by breed. All-white cats are uncommon, which is good, because they may have more health issues than cats of other colours. They also can sunburn.

TAIL: The domestic, or house, cat is the only cat species that can hold its tail up straight while walking. Lions, tigers, and other wild cats either hold their tails horizontally or tucked between their legs when they walk.

NAILS: Most cats have five toes on each front foot and four toes on the back. Some cats, known as polydactyls, have four to eight extra toes. The sharp, hooked claws on the end of each toe can be retracted, or pulled up out of the way, when a cat isn't hunting or fighting.

Abyssinian

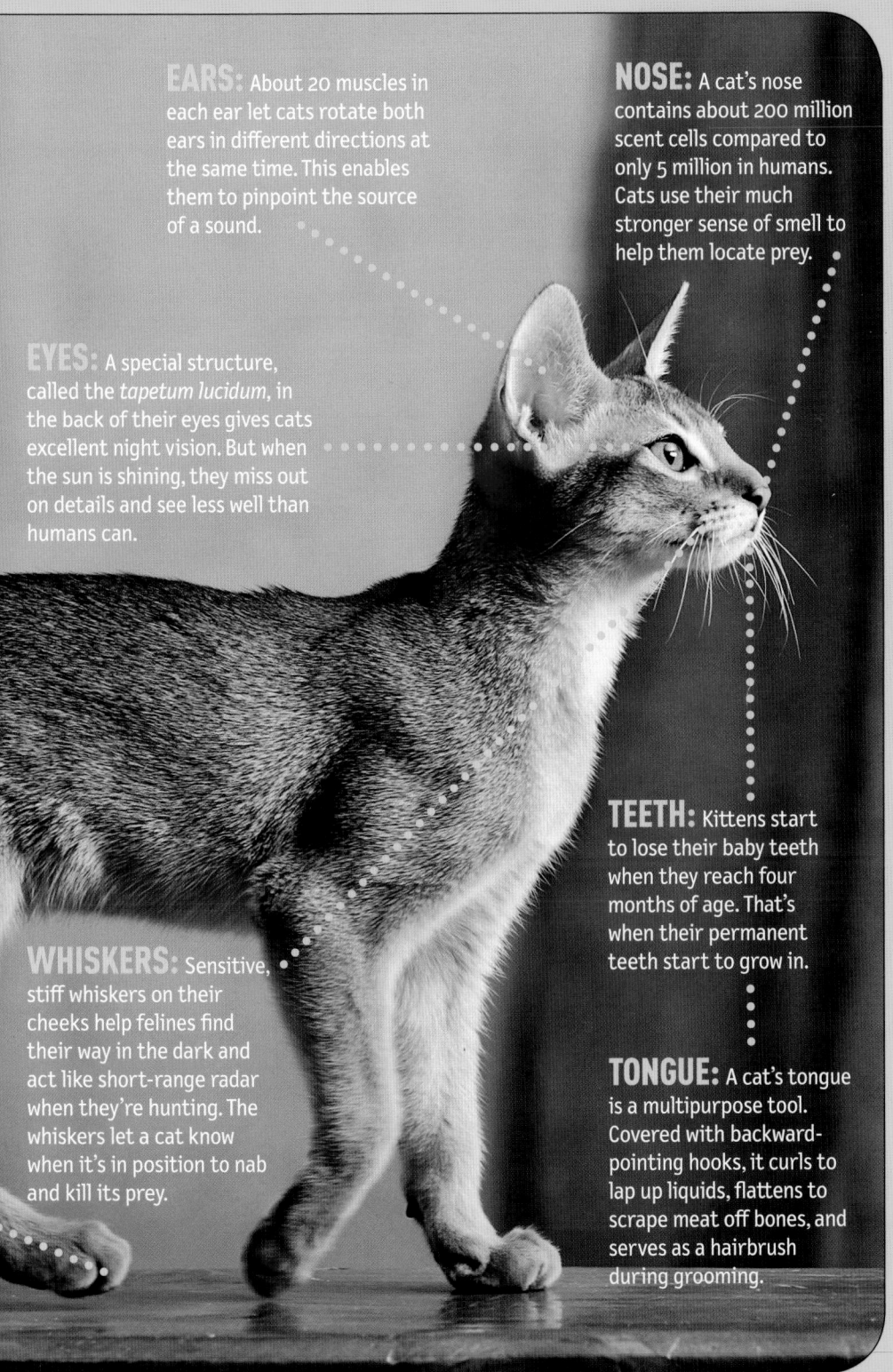

EARS: About 20 muscles in each ear let cats rotate both ears in different directions at the same time. This enables them to pinpoint the source of a sound.

NOSE: A cat's nose contains about 200 million scent cells compared to only 5 million in humans. Cats use their much stronger sense of smell to help them locate prey.

EYES: A special structure, called the *tapetum lucidum*, in the back of their eyes gives cats excellent night vision. But when the sun is shining, they miss out on details and see less well than humans can.

TEETH: Kittens start to lose their baby teeth when they reach four months of age. That's when their permanent teeth start to grow in.

WHISKERS: Sensitive, stiff whiskers on their cheeks help felines find their way in the dark and act like short-range radar when they're hunting. The whiskers let a cat know when it's in position to nab and kill its prey.

TONGUE: A cat's tongue is a multipurpose tool. Covered with backward-pointing hooks, it curls to lap up liquids, flattens to scrape meat off bones, and serves as a hairbrush during grooming.

CaTs:
ALL IN THE
FaMILY

If they held a reunion, invitations would go to over 40 branches of the Family Felidae, and descendants would come from around the world. Though cat taxonomy frequently changes, scientists have currently classified all these cat cousins into 13 groups, based on their DNA. Family "spokes-cats" from 11 of these are listed below. The others include Profelis and Puma.

MARBLED CAT
Indonesia

KNOWN FOR: Spectacular bushy tail as long as the cat's whole body

GROUP: *Pardofelis*

NUMBER IN GROUP: **1**

CANADA LYNX
Canada and Alaska

KNOWN FOR: Large, furry paws that act like snowshoes

GROUP: *Lynx*

NUMBER IN GROUP: **4**

NORTHEASTERN TIGRINA
Brazil

KNOWN FOR: The world's "newest cat", discovered in 2013

GROUP: *Leopardus*

NUMBER IN GROUP: **7**

CARACAL
Africa

KNOWN FOR: High jumper that lives in the desert

GROUP: *Caracal*

NUMBER IN GROUP: **1**

SUNDALAND CLOUDED LEOPARD
Borneo and Sumatra

KNOWN FOR: Spends most of its time in the tree canopy

GROUP: *Neofelis*

NUMBER IN GROUP: **2**

CHEETAH
Africa and Iran

KNOWN FOR: World's fastest land animal—can go from standing still to 60 mph (97 kph) in 3 seconds

GROUP: *Acinonyx*

NUMBER IN GROUP: **1**

AFRICAN LION
Sub-Saharan Africa

KNOWN FOR: Its great roar that can be heard up to 5 miles (8 km) away

GROUP: *Panthera*

NUMBER IN GROUP: **4**

SERVAL
African savanna

KNOWN AS: "Giraffe cat" due to very long neck

GROUP: *Leptailurus*

NUMBER IN GROUP: **1**

ASIATIC GOLDEN CAT
Asia, China, and the Himalaya

KNOWN AS: "Fire tiger"

GROUP: *Catopuma*

NUMBER IN GROUP: **2**

FISHING CAT
India, China, and other countries in Southeast Asia

KNOWN FOR: Partly webbed paws used for swimming and catching fish

GROUP: *Prionailurus*

NUMBER IN GROUP: **5**

HOUSE CAT
Everywhere!

KNOWN FOR: Purring and snuggling

GROUP: *Felis*

NUMBER IN GROUP: **7**

SOME PEOPLE CLASSIFY themselves as dog lovers. Others prefer cats. Together, dogs and cats are the most popular pets in the world today. But make no mistake. From the sounds they make to the games they play, dogs and cats are very different species. Yet, despite their differences, almost everyone knows a pooch and a puss that adore each other, maybe as much as we humans adore them. Opposites attract, and here's a chart to prove it.

Siamese with
a cocker spaniel

CaTS vs. DoGS

Are skilled hunters.	Are bacon beggars.
Demand to be paid.	Will work for praise.
Can make more than 100 different sounds.	Can make more than 100 different facial expressions.
Are hard to figure out.	Are easy to understand.
Are bred solely for looks.	Are bred for what they can do.
Enjoy being alone.	Love hanging with the crowd.
Are fickle at best.	Are loyal to a fault.
Try to hide how they feel.	Wear their hearts on their tails.
Are sleepy couch potatoes.	Are energetic workaholics.
Often climb up curtains.	Sometimes eat the curtains.
Are born to be wild.	Are born totally tame.
Think, "What's in it for me?"	Say, "Tell me what you want."
Are hard (but possible!) to train.	Are easy to train.
Like to sleep on your head.	Like to sleep on your bed.

Cat TALK QUIZ

Test your kitty know-how! Match each cat's posture to the correct emotion. Fill in each box with the correct letter. (Check your answers below.)

1. RELAXED "It's a calm, quiet day in the neighbourhood."

2. ANGRY "Get away! Or I'll make you leave!"

3. FRIENDLY "Hi, there. You can pet me if you want."

4. AFRAID "Come one step closer, and I'll bolt! I swear I will!"

5. ANXIOUS "Uh oh. I don't think I'm going to like this."

6. PLAYFUL "Come on. Shake a leg and play with me."

All cats pictured here are domestic shorthairs, except for C, which is a Peterbald.

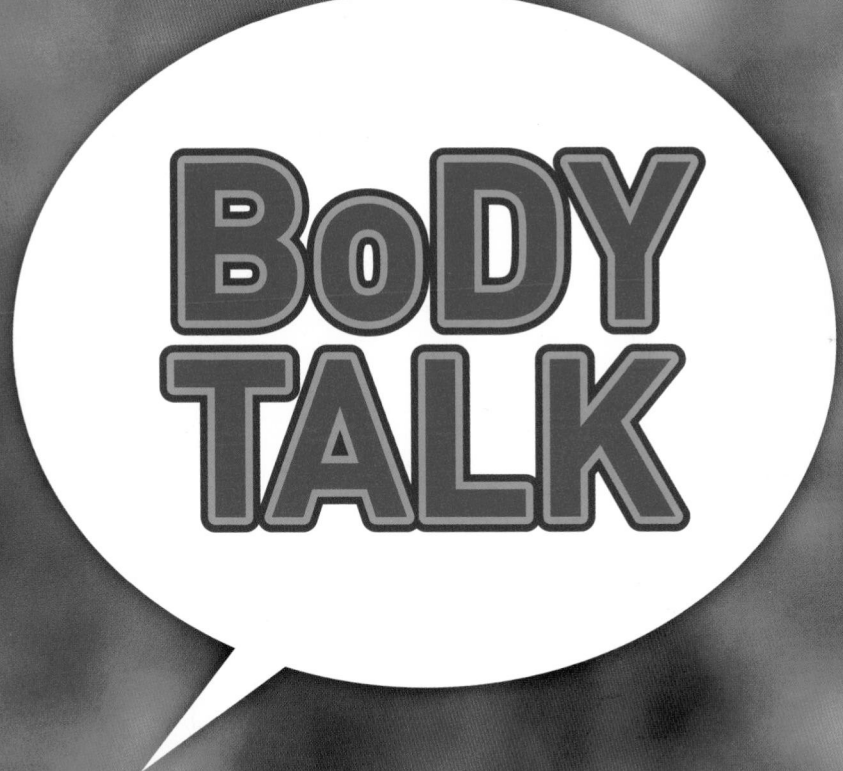

BODY TALK

CATS ARE ON A ROLL. All around the globe, cats now rank as the most popular companion animal. We admire their strong, athletic bodies and love to stroke their beautiful soft fur. It makes us feel good when a friendly kitty purrs contentedly, rubs against our legs, or snuggles in our laps. But let's get one thing straight: Cats are not dogs!

They look, act, and (we're pretty sure) think different. There are good reasons for this. Besides being a completely separate species, domestic cats only recently arrived on the scene. Humans began taming and living with dogs about 12,000 years ago. But another 8,000 years went by before we started keeping cats as pets. That means cats haven't had enough time to evolve into a tamer, more domesticated version of themselves.

Whereas dogs depend on us to take care of them, cats remain mostly wild. Being self-reliant, they hide their feelings. Unless you know exactly what to look for, a happy cat and a miserable one can look much the same. But cats do communicate somewhat through body language. And you can learn to understand it! Keep reading to find out how.

THERE GOES CHESTER, SNIFFING MRS. GRUNDY'S BIN AGAIN.

DR. GARY'S VET TIPS

UNFORTUNATELY, BEING up high isn't always as safe as cats think it is. City cats sometimes suffer from "high-rise syndrome". That's what we call it when flat-dwelling cats jump or fall from balconies, windows, or fire escapes. Cat owners who live on upper floors should reinforce balcony railings with chicken wire and make sure their windows have tight-fitting screens. Only the luckiest of cats can survive the plunge.

KING OF the HILL

You've seen them … cats in high places. Perched on tree branches, prowling along the rafters of cow barns, even sitting on top of bookcases and refrigerators. Cats are good climbers and high jumpers. So it's no mystery how they get up there. But the question is why?

There are two reasons. First of all, everybody likes a room with a view, especially cats. Being up high lets these furry busybodies watch both our comings and goings and those of rival cats. And they can do it without risking any unpleasant confrontations. Cats will go to great lengths (and heights!) to avoid a cat fight.

Second, it's a safety issue. In the wild, a leopard scales a tree to get out of danger. A nervous house cat bolts up the stairs. One of the best things you can do for your kitty is to give him several choice perching spots. A deep windowsill; a high-backed, overstuffed chair; or a sleeping pillow placed on top of a cupboard work well. If you have more than one cat, each needs a place. And just like a couple of kids, who both want to sit up front in the car, your cats are likely to wrangle over who gets the top spot.

A cat can jump about five to seven times his own height.

European shorthair

WAIT and WATCH

"Never give up." That's good advice. But it's wasted on cats. Cats *always* keep trying. Suppose yours likes to lie on the kitchen table. You know what that's like. Kitty jumps up. You put her down on the floor. Kitty jumps up again. You put her back down. And so it goes, on and on. Either you give in and let her do what she wants or you shut her out of the room. And then she might yowl!

Cats are amazingly persistent. All that built-in stick-to-itiveness comes from the way they hunt. Rather than chase down prey like wolves do, cats lie in wait and ambush it. Masters of the sneak attack, house cats are born with the rules of the hunt pre-programmed in their brains:

1. Wait and watch.
2. Crouch and stalk.
3. Pounce!
4. Grab the prey with one paw.
5. Kill the prey by biting its neck.
6. Rip and swallow. It's suppertime.

This is why cats can sit patiently outside a mouse hole for hours watching for lunch to appear. Then, when it does … "Yum!" But cats will watch and wait even when there is no possibility of food at the end. That's because watchful waiting is the first step in the hunting sequence. Once a flutter or some other quick movement triggers the instinct, cats are hard-wired to follow through.

Some cats get **frustrated** watching birds they can't catch, **but not Snoopy, a black cat from Dunkirk, Maryland, U.S.A.** She regularly watches **nature shows on TV.**

STALKING

Slow and steady wins the race—and catches the mouse. Have you ever seen a cat creeping along with his belly almost hitting the ground? His whole body is tense. He moves stealthily, padding on soft paws, with staring eyes and ears pointed forward. Cats do much of their hunting at night. And they have a blind spot under their nose. So, as a cat closes in on his prey, the whiskers on his cheeks send signals to his brain telling him exactly where that prey is.

Scientists have discovered that even blind cats can catch mice, proving that their whiskers really do have an important part to play when stalking prey. The signals from their whiskers help them locate prey, enabling them to pounce immediately when they come into contact with a mouse.

It is by combining information from their eyes, ears, nose, and whiskers that cats manage to hunt as well as they do after dark. When the prey is loose, the hunt may take several minutes. During that time, only the twitching of a cat's tail betrays his excitement. But sooner or later, his head will start swaying from side to side. When that happens, his prey is near. So get ready. He's about to pounce!

Cats and elephants are both **digitigrade** walkers, which means they walk on their **toes.**

BYE-BYE, BIRDIE.

DR. GARY'S VET TIPS

CATS ARE excellent hunters in almost any setting. But that doesn't mean you can just dump a cat in some strange place, drive away, and he'll be okay. He won't be. If you leave him by a farm or someplace where there are other cats around, the other cats will usually drive him off. A former pet, left in an unfamiliar environment, won't find enough food. Most die from starvation, disease, exposure to the cold, predators like coyotes, or traffic. So don't be cruel. Try to find your cat a good home. As a last resort, if no one you know can take him, bring him to an animal shelter.

POUNCING

He watches. He crouches. He pounces! (But he may not score.) Pouncing is the third step in the feline rules of the hunt. And there's a trick to it. A cat must aim his pounce perfectly. If he misses the mouse, he can't just "try, try again". He usually has to go back to the beginning and sit and watch. That's because a cat's six-part hunting sequence is what scientists call a motor pattern. A motor pattern is a series of actions that must be done in a specific order.

It's like when the bowler in a cricket match bowls a ball that the batter can't hit and the wicket-keeper can't catch. He won't immediately bowl another.

First, he'll rub the ball, glance at the wicket-keeper, methodically walk back to his bowling mark, and so on. Whatever his routine, the bowler needs to repeat it step by step. A hunting cat does the same. Of course, by the time kitty does all that, his meal is long gone.

Bowlers also must practise hard to hone their skills. So must cats. You can help yours by dragging a string tied to a stick along the floor or tossing paper balls for him to pounce on. Even well-fed indoor cats love to play-hunt. It helps satisfy that strong, inner urge they were born with but never get to use.

When outside fending for themselves, **domestic** cats hunt an average of **10 mice** a day ... but they only catch **3**.

GAME ON

Like you, kittens just want to have fun. They love to run and chase, pounce and wrestle, attack and retreat. But these are the same behaviours cats use when hunting and fighting. So how does one kitten know whether another kitten has fighting or playing on her mind?

It turns out that kittens have special signals to tell each other just that. One kitten will roll over on her back with a relaxed look on her face. Then another kitten will lean back on her hind legs and raise her front paws in the air. Or it might be the other way around. Either way, that does it. Let the games begin!

Kitties learn these play signals from their littermates. And they learn them when they're tiny, between three and seven weeks old. If they are separated from their littermates during that important time, they will never learn these signals. Although they will probably play with toys, they'll never be able to play with other cats.

One word of warning: An adult cat that rears up on his hind legs isn't always feeling playful. He may be downright grumpy. So make sure his tail isn't twitching before you reach out. Otherwise, you might get swatted.

Some of the best cat toys are free: a paper bag or crumpled-up newspaper on the floor.

HIDING

 Pepper, a tabby cat, lived with a Keeshond puppy named Buffy. The two animals got along well and often played together. Buffy never hurt Pepper, but sometimes she took Pepper's whole head into her mouth. Wade, their teenage owner, thought Pepper needed a time-out spot or safety zone. So he cut a small opening into the hinged lid of the cardboard box his trainers came in and set it on a bookshelf.

Pepper adopted it immediately. Whenever the playing got too rough, she ran to her kitty-cave. She pushed up the hinged cover by poking her nose into the hole and jumped inside. The cover would close down over her, and she'd stay in there (often with her tail hanging out the hole!) until she sensed that the coast was clear.

When feeling stressed, a cat's first response is always to run and hide. These furry scaredy-cats feel most secure in small, dark, quiet places. And it's always better to provide them with a safe haven yourself. It could be an upside-down box with a hole in the side, an empty paper bag, or a cubbyhole cut in the skirting board. Left to find their own spots, cats often choose dangerous places where they could get trapped. They crawl inside cupboards, suitcases, dresser drawers, and washing machines. Cats can even get stuck inside walls during construction projects.

DR. GARY'S VET TIPS

WE NEED to worry about cats and cars. Besides the risk of being run over, cats love sleeping in or underneath parked vehicles. In the winter, they can seek out tyre wells or crawl under the bonnet for warmth. Come morning, many are horribly injured when their unsuspecting owners leave for work. The hiding cats either get cut by turning fan belts or thrown out of the wheel wells at high speed. We also need to check our cars in the summer, because cats will sometimes sun themselves on the roof.

Natasha, a California, U.S.A., kitty, hid in the washing machine and somehow survived an entire 35-minute wash cycle before emerging, soaked and shocked, but sweet-smelling.

YOU'LL NEVER FIND ME IN HERE!

HEADBUTTING and BODY RUBBING

Whoa! Your kitty just bumped you on the forehead—on purpose. Now she's rubbing the side of her body against your legs. What's up with all this? Cat owners usually think their pet wants food. And some do, because they have learned that rubbing gets it for them. But what makes cats rub and headbutt in the first place? The strange behaviour has mystified scientists for years.

Because cats have scent glands on their cheeks, jaw, and around their tail, most scientists think cats are spreading their scent: a sort of kitty perfume that only cats can smell. But cat researcher John Bradshaw has a new idea. He has seen cats body rub other cats and even dogs. Yet doing this doesn't get them food or anything else in return. What's more, cats don't sniff when they body rub. They seem not to care if an enemy cat has already contaminated us with its scent. And cats only headbutt and body rub people and animals that they like. All this has convinced Bradshaw that our favourite furballs don't have any ulterior motive at all. He believes body rubbing is simply a cat's way of showing affection. Is he right? Maybe. But more studies are needed to be sure.

All cats, except the hairless Sphynx, leave hair on furniture and clothes, but the Cornish Rex sheds the least.

Cornish Rex

WELCOME HOME! IT'S GREAT TO HAVE YOU BACK.

HERE!
I SAVED THE
BEST PART
FOR YOU!

GIFT GIVING

Ewww! Your cat leaves a dead mouse on the front steps. Or worse yet, she trots right up to you and drops a still-wiggling one at your feet. Cats are born to hunt. It's how they feed their kittens. But, besides bringing home take-away, mama cats use live prey to show their kittens how to hunt themselves.

"Okay," you say. "But what's with my cat? She doesn't have kittens." Some scientists believe your cat feels so close to you that she thinks *you* are her kitten. Other experts think that's silly because you're so much bigger.

It's far more likely that well-fed pet cats behave like human hunters. Human hunters don't shoot a rabbit and scoff it right down. They bring their trophy home to show their family and eat it later. Even mountain lions drag their prey into the woods, cover it with leaves, and nibble it little by little. So it stands to reason that some house cats return with their catch. Then they may abandon it in favor of the yummier morsels waiting in their dish.

If your cat brings you an unwanted gift, don't scold her. Praise her hunting ability. After all, maybe she caught that creature in your kitchen! Then slip your hand into a plastic sandwich bag, pick up the mess, and throw it away. Be thankful that you don't have to eat it either.

Towser, a female cat in Perthshire, Scotland, holds the world record for being the best mouser. In 23 years, she caught 28,899 mice.

IT'S HARD
WORK ALWAYS
LOOKING
MY BEST.

DR. GARY'S VET TIPS

MOST CATS love being brushed, and regular brushing reduces the number of hairballs they produce. It also stimulates oil production in their skin for a healthier coat. But if your cat needs a bath, and cats sometimes do, take him to a professional groomer. Professional groomers also help if a cat's fur gets badly matted. If your cat is particularly matted, a groomer can give him a "lion cut". A lion cut is when the groomer shears the cat everywhere except for his paws, tail tip, head, and neck. It's similar to a "poodle cut" for dogs. And getting rid of that matted hair probably makes cats feel as good as humans do after visiting the beauty salon.

HAIR CARE

"Mirror, mirror on the wall. Who's the fairest of them all?" With cats, it's difficult to say. Those delicate kitty faces and striking fur coats make them all beautiful. What's more, they're always *purr*-fectly groomed.

Cats comb and clean their coat with their tongue. That's right. A cat's tongue is like a mini-hairbrush. It's covered with backward-facing bristles. When scraped across her fur, these bristles untangle snarls and pull out fleas and loose hairs. Only trouble is, kitty has no choice but to swallow that stuff. Usually this is okay. The hair passes through her digestive system without a problem. But not always. Sometimes things do get a little *hairy*.

That's when balls of hair form in a cat's stomach, and the cat throws them up—usually on the living room carpet. This doesn't hurt the cat, but it drives some owners nuts. The problem gets much worse with long-haired cats, like Persians and Himalayans. Despite these cats' best efforts, their fur gets tangled and matted and they get lots of hairballs, unless an owner brushes them every day.

Some people go so far as to send their high-maintenance mousers to feline beauty salons. There, pampered pets put up their paws and let professional groomers do their "dirty work". But don't worry. Most kitties don't need all that. Your cat considers being in your lap the lap of luxury.

At some **kitty spas,** cats are treated to catnip tea, as well as hot towel wraps, facials, and fancy hairdos.

LICKING

Have you ever heard the saying, "You scratch my back and I'll scratch yours"? Well, substitute "lick" for "scratch" and it applies equally well to cats.

Mother cats lick their babies all the time. They do it to keep them clean, but kittens love it! Her rough tongue feels good on their fur. It comforts them and makes them feel safe. Even as adults, cats lick themselves to calm down after a scary or upsetting experience. Licking reduces tension. In much the same way that a nervous human might keep checking his mobile phone, licking gives a nervous cat something to do. It also helps cats cool down in the heat and actually lowers their heart rate.

Besides licking themselves, adult cats also sometimes lick each other, but only if they're related or are good friends. No meanies or strangers allowed. A grooming pair takes turns licking behind each other's ears and other places that are hard to reach. But that's not the main reason they do it. They do it because mutual licking strengthens their relationship. It helps them bond.

In fact, licking may even help cats bond with us. Many experts think cats consider stroking a form of licking, which could explain why your kitty licks you in return. Or he could be apologizing for ignoring you earlier. Scientists aren't sure. But whatever his reason for doing it, licking is always meant as a good thing—even if that scratchy tongue hurts a bit.

Cats spend **one-third** or more of their **waking hours** **grooming.**

Highland folds

British shorthair

AHH. NOW A LITTLE MORE TO THE RIGHT, PLEASE.

DR. GARY'S VET TIPS

SOME CATS groom too much and end up with bald spots or red, inflamed patches of skin. Vets call this psychogenic alopecia, and it's all too common. It's a compulsive behaviour, like humans who chew their fingernails, and is usually caused by anxiety or stress.

Removing the cause of the stress is the best treatment. The cause for cats, 90 percent of the time, is other cats! To alleviate stress, all cats need their own space from time to time. If you can't provide that for your stressed-out cat, your vet might want to discuss putting him on anti-anxiety medicine.

38

SOCIAL ROLL

Stop, flop, and roll. That's what Hobbs, a young gray and black rescue kitty, did every time he greeted a member of his human family. Talk about acting laid-back! He would run down the path and collapse at their feet. This endearing behaviour is called a social roll. It's a kitty's way of saying he wants to interact with you. Hobbs hoped you would slide your hands underneath him and scoop him up into your arms.

Kittens do the same thing when they want to play. A dog says, "Let's play!" by putting his elbows on the ground and sticking his bottom in the air. A kitten goes "belly-up". That's the signal for another kitten to stand up on his hind legs. Then the two lock bodies and tumble over and over in an adorable fun-filled frenzy.

But just know a cat's social roll is very different from a dog that turns up his belly to you. Our dogs love to have their bellies rubbed. Cats don't. Any cat that dares expose his belly to you is saying he feels safe and trusts you completely. If you violate that trust by touching his tummy, watch out! He's likely to defend himself by grabbing your hand with all four paws and clawing it to bits. Better just to talk sweetly to him instead.

Forty percent of cats are right-pawed, 20 percent are left-pawed, and 40 percent use both paws equally.

Burmese

Maine Coon

RUBBING NOSES

People kiss "hello". Cats rub noses. Sometimes cats try to greet us the same way, but being on the short side, they can't reach that high. So they may stand up on their hind legs to get closer. At this point, some knowing people pick up their kitty so she can reach. Others crouch down and meet their kitty face to face.

After the nose rub, cats also do like dogs and take turns sniffing each other's rear ends. Thank goodness they don't try doing that with us! But the fact that nose rubbing is followed by sniffing tells us that there is more going on than it looks like at first. Sure, it probably feels good when kitties gently rub noses. But greeting has a deeper meaning. It transfers scent and gives cats important information about each other. Cats recognize friends and family by the way they smell. They also like to have their housemates and their home all smelling the same. When all those smells match, it's called having a "family odour".

Many cats sniff and rub their people, other cats, and the furniture every day so as to keep that family odour in place. But they don't rub every Max, Jack, and Bella they happen to meet. Cats only nose rub animals and humans they know and love—like you!

Eric the barn cat climbs the enclosure fence **every day** to rub noses with his buddy, a quarter horse named Topper.

SLUMBER PARTY

Beautiful dreamers. That certainly describes cats. They can curl up anywhere—in a cardboard box, on the sofa back, or on your computer keyboard. They prefer snoozing somewhere up high and love warm, comfy spots. But it's safety first, which for one long-haired stray meant sleeping on a bumpy pile of firewood. But wherever they pick, cats look so comfortable that we can't bear to disturb them.

A cat that feels completely at ease closes his eyes, relaxes his ears, and curls his front paws. Those upturned paws show that he feels safe and isn't about to run off.

Healthy adult cats are the Sleeping Beauties of the animal kingdom. They often spend two-thirds of their life sleeping, up to 18 hours a day. Some scientists think they may sleep so much because a cat's hunting style requires short bursts of explosive energy. But nobody knows for sure.

What we do know is that cats divide their sleep time into many *catnaps*. Bored cats sleep more than cats that play and interact with people. And cats probably dream. Studies show that cats sleep in two stages—deep sleep and light sleep—like humans do. And their brain wave patterns are similar to ours. Given that sleeping cats often twitch their ears and wiggle their whiskers, the only question left is what they're dreaming about. Any ideas?

Studies show that **stroking a cat** or just watching one sleep **lowers blood pressure** in humans.

WHAT IS THIS CaT SAYING?

The Scenario

Olivia doesn't look like a thief. But this sweet-faced black-and-white outdoor kitty regularly steals from her neighbours. It all started one day in 2009. Olivia trotted into owner Anne Weizel's backyard with something in her mouth. It was a rolled-up mini-toolkit containing wrenches, pliers, and a screwdriver.

Before long, Weizel began finding gardening gloves on her front steps. Every day for three months straight more gloves appeared, some with price tags still attached. It's been many years, but Olivia's crime spree persists. Besides gardening gloves, her loot includes stuffed animals, rolls of toilet paper, Christmas ornaments, a lady's bra, and kids' flip-flops—over 700 items in all! Once, she dragged home a large and very heavy man's shoe. Hours later, she brought in the other!

You Be the Expert

So what's going on here? What could this cat be thinking? Why has she turned to a life of crime?

Cats hunt. That's what they do. So this is entirely natural behaviour. The only thing weird about it is her choice of prey, and probably not for the reason you think. A cat's hunting instinct is triggered by movement. But Olivia is stalking "prey" that's already "dead".

It looks as if this cat has figured out a way to have her prey and "eat" it, too. Hunting is risky. A captured bird could poke her in the eye with its beak. A rat could bite her ears or face. But sandals and gardening gloves don't fight back. Olivia doesn't need to hunt to survive. This way she can enjoy the excitement of watching and waiting, stalking, pouncing, and grabbing her prey without having to actually kill it—which is much safer.

Jail, Bail, or Kitty Reform School?

Olivia's burglar behaviour is the talk of her Milford, Connecticut, U.S.A., town. But she really isn't so much stealing as showing off. She gets to act like a great hunter and bring home her trophies to Anne, who picks her up and tells her what a good kitty she is. Then Anne tosses Olivia's treasures in the washing machine and puts them in the "Lost and Found" box she keeps for her neighbours to "paw" through.

The only way Anne could stop this behaviour is by locking Olivia inside at night. But that might cause her kitty serious anxiety and could lead to other issues. No, Olivia doesn't deserve jail for this. In fact, Anne probably prefers her object "thievery" to having dead mice or headless shrews dropped off in her living room. Wouldn't you?

HIGH FIVE: HOW TO RAISE A COOL CAT

Teach this trick first. It prepares your cat to learn more.

 1 Buy an inexpensive clicker training kit at a pet store. Cats are harder to train than dogs, because they don't care about pleasing humans. So this little noisemaker helps.

 2 Hold training sessions right before mealtime, when kitty is hungry. Grab a handful of really yummy treats, like deli meat or pieces of canned tuna meant as people food.

 3 Take your cat to a quiet room and sit on the floor with him. Hold the clicker in one hand. Grasp a treat between the fingers of your other hand.

 4 Jiggle the treat in front of your cat. The second he swats for it, click and give it to him. Timing matters. You want your cat to associate the clicking sound with receiving his reward.

 5 Do this every day for ten minutes. Soon your kitty will high five you whenever you click, even when you have no treats.

Persian

REaD MY FACE

MOTHER NATURE designed cats to hunt. She gave them sharp hearing, keen eyesight, large brains, powerful jaws, and pointed teeth. Most domestic cats looked alike. But then humans got involved and began breeding cats to look pretty. Now pet cats come in many varieties. Shorthaired kitties usually have big heads with rectangular faces. Their ears are set far apart. Longhaired cats, like Persians, have round, flat faces with squished noses. Siamese cats had round faces 100 years ago, but no longer. Today's Siamese sport wedge-shaped faces with pointy chins.

More important than shape is a cat's facial expression—or, rather, lack of it. Cats are like poker players. They hide their thoughts and feelings. That's because, in the wild, male cats live alone and must compete with each other for food and mates. Any cat that reveals what he's thinking makes himself easy to beat. So cats are deliberately inscrutable. Sometimes the only clue we get is a twitching ear or blinking eye. And we must look closely to see that!

DR. GARY'S VET TIPS

CATS' EYES GLOW in the dark, making them look spooky at night. Because they hunt in dim light, they need to have supersharp vision. So cats have developed an extra layer of tissue behind the retina, which is in the back of the eye. This extra tissue is called the *tapetum lucidum,* Latin for "bright carpet". It acts like a mirror, reflecting light that was not absorbed the first time it passed through the retina, greatly improving a cat's night vision. It also ruins many good pet photos, by making a cat's eyes shine!

**YOUR SECRET
IS SAFE
WITH ME.**

SLOW BLINKING

A cat's eyes are open windows into his heart. By looking into our kitty's eyes, we can tell much about what he's thinking and feeling. But the signals are subtle, so you need to know what you're looking for.

One of the sweetest signs, yet one that is easily missed, is the slow blink of one or both eyes. That's right. When a cat blinks at you, it actually means something. Between two people, a wink is a loving gesture—a sign of affection or solidarity. It usually means that you share something in common—perhaps a goal or a happy secret.

A slow blink from a cat is a lot like that. It means the cat feels relaxed and friendly and likes being with you. And it still means this, even if she blinks and turns her head away. She's not rejecting you. Quite the opposite. She's saying that she feels so safe and comfortable when you're around that she doesn't need to stay on alert. Blinking is like a kitty kiss!

And you can prove it. The next time you and your kitty are just lazing around, make sure she's looking, and then give her a wink. If you're lucky, she'll "kiss" you back.

All cats, no matter their breed, are born with blue eyes. Their true colour appears at about 12 weeks.

Persian

WIDE-EYED STARE

The eyes have it. Or so say scientists, who claim humans are drawn to faces with large eyes. That's part of the reason why we fall for babies … and cats. Cats have huge eyes, especially for such little heads. A cat's eyes are almost as big as yours. But because cats hunt, their eyes are designed differently. For one thing, their colour vision is poor. Most colours look faded, and they can't see red or orange at all.

But, more important is the fact that cats' eyes don't focus very well. This may be because the lenses work differently or simply because focusing such big eyes is hard work. Either way their world looks blurry. Except, and this is a big exception, when something moves within "pouncing distance".

Let a mouse skitter or a robin hop past and those relaxed eyes zero right in. Moving prey doesn't even need to be in front of a cat for him to see it. Cats have superior peripheral vision. They can spot the tiniest movement taking place halfway around the sides of their heads.

So if your cat looks wide-eyed, he's interested in something. And if you're wiggling your fingers or toes, be prepared. It's very likely that something is you!

Cats' eyes come in
three shapes:
almond, round, and oval.

PUPILS LIKE SLITS

Sunglasses on cats? It's not likely, because cats don't need them. True, their eyes are extremely sensitive to light. They have to be, or cats wouldn't be able to see well enough to hunt after dark. The secret lies in having pupils that automatically react to changing light. The pupil is the black circle in the centre of the eye that light passes through. Like us, the darker it gets, the bigger a cat's pupils get. It's like opening the curtains.

During the day, when cats go out in the sun, their pupils get smaller. If the sun is really bright, their pupils shrink to vertical slits. That's like closing the blinds.

Some evening, after the sun goes down, take your cat into a semi-dark room. Sit under a lamp with him on your lap. Then turn on the lamp and watch what happens to his eyes. The pupils will contract to slits the size of buttonholes. If they didn't, the strong light could damage his eyesight. When you turn the lamp off, his pupils will dilate, or get big again—maybe as big as a five-pence coin.

So what does all this mean to you? The size of a cat's pupils is a clue to what he's thinking. If his pupils get big, even though there's lots of light, watch out. He's either angry or planning to pounce!

A cat can see about **six times better** than a person can at **night.**

DROOPY, HALF-CLOSED EYELIDS

"Night, night. Sleep tight." Or maybe not. Just because a cat is lying there with eyes half shut doesn't mean he's heading off to dreamland. It might just be that the light is too bright. Honest. Cats' eyes are so easily damaged that nature provided several means of protection. The first is automatic. In bright sun, the round black pupils in the centre of a kitty's eyes instantly narrow to slits. When that's not enough, cats can lower their upper eyelid and raise the bottom one. Then they peer out of the area in between.

And that's not all. Nature also gave cats a third eyelid. It's called the nictitating membrane, and most people don't even know it exists. It only shows itself in Siamese, Burmese, or Tonkinese cats, or in sick cats that need to be taken to the vet. Otherwise, this pale pink membrane stays hidden in the corner of a cat's eye. But it acts like a secret weapon. If a sharp stick threatens to injure a hunting cat's eye, this third eyelid sweeps across like a windscreen wiper and clears it away.

So don't be too quick to assume that your sleepy-looking kitty is a total couch potato. Could be he's just resting his eyes.

Cats are **nearsighted.** What humans can see clearly at a distance will look **blurry** to a cat.

WOULD SOMEBODY PLEASE TURN OFF THAT LIGHT?!

DR. GARY'S VET TIPS

LIKE HUMANS, cats lose vision as they age. The change is gradual and can be hard to detect. But if you have an elderly cat, here are some warning signs: The lenses of his eyes look cloudy or white. Your cat is missing jumps. For example, he might try to leap from the floor to your desk and slip back because he fails to land with all four feet. Or he may have trouble batting around a toy mouse. This is because the toy is silent, and his hearing can't compensate for his loss of sight. If you see changes like these, bring your cat to the vet. But don't despair. Most cats can adjust.

STARING

You've probably been in a staring contest—when two kids lock eyes and try to stare each other down. Whoever blinks first loses. Well, cats do the same thing. Only with them, it isn't a game. It's deadly serious.

Cats stare intently at their prey when they're on the hunt. And they use staring whenever they want to threaten or dominate another creature. Suppose a cat encounters a dog or a neighbourhood cat that he doesn't like or doesn't know. He's likely to sit down and stare directly at whatever he thinks is invading his turf. That hard stare is a warning: Put up your paws or get out!

So it's only natural that cats consider staring "rude" and find it intimidating to be stared at themselves. This is why it's wise to avoid looking any cat right in the eyes. And it's especially important if you're dealing with a scaredy-cat. If fact, some people suggest that if you wear glasses, it might help to take them off. Then your eyes won't appear so large and scary.

The thing to remember is this: If you don't stare at your cat, maybe he won't stare at you. That should keep everyone happy.

WATCH IT, BUSTER. ONE WRONG MOVE AND...

An unusual tortoiseshell cat
named **Venus**
has different
coloured eyes;
one is green
and the other is blue.

PERKED EARS

Close your eyes and picture a cat. She probably has a relaxed face and gently perked ears. That's how our beloved pets look most of the time. Their ears are standing up, although still bendy, and facing toward the front. Or they may be tipped slightly to the sides.

But what a difference a minute makes. Feline hunters depend on their hearing as well as their eyesight to track prey. So all it takes is a rustle in the grass or a high-pitched squeak from behind the woodwork. Faster than you can say "rodent stew", a cat can switch from being on standby to full attention. Her eyes will open wide, and her ears will stiffen. Once fully erect, her ears may continue to face the front, or they may swivel right or left, in the direction of the sound. The change is subtle. You have to look closely to see it. But the position of a cat's ears is one of the most reliable clues any cat gives to how she is feeling. And if she's feeling like hunting, that's good to know. A cat on a mission will not welcome any interference, whether from you or someone else. Better just to wish her luck and let her go.

One company sells computerized cat ears for people. Controlled by brain waves, the ears perk up when you're alert and droop when you're bored.

FLATTENED EARS

Beware a cat with flattened ears! A scared cat, or a cat facing a fight, will turn his ears back and flatten them on top of his head. Sometimes the flattened ears practically disappear into his fur. Other times they stick out like little airplane wings. Either way, it's a good defense. Cat fights are vicious. Both the winner and the loser can end up with claw wounds or bites taken out of their ears.

There is one unusual breed of cat, called the Scottish Fold, that can't flatten its ears, no matter how frightened it is. That's because its ears already lie flat! The first feline that had this feature was a barn cat born in Scotland in 1961. Today, cats of this type are bred mostly in the United States.

Scottish Fold kittens are born with normal-looking pointed ears, but two to four weeks later their ears begin bending over like wilted flowers. By three months, the kittens' ears are so small and lying so close to their head that they look like little owls.

Some people refuse to breed Scottish Folds because the flattened ears cover the ear canals, making it hard to hear. It's the same reason why frightened or fighting cats don't keep their ears down any longer than necessary. They pop them right back up for fear of missing something.

I'M WARNING YOU! DON'T COME ANY CLOSER!

DR. GARY'S VET TIPS

DEAFNESS IN cats is largely due to old age or kittens being born that way. Blue-eyed, all-white cats are almost always deaf. And there is no cure. All we can do is make life easier for them. Since a deaf cat can't hear you coming, he might be easily startled. So try not to approach him from behind or touch him when he's sleeping. Some owners teach their deaf cats to come by following a flashlight beam. On another note, it's a good idea to check your cat's ears. They should be clean and pink. If you see any redness or discharge, take her to the vet.

A fear of cats
is called **ailurophobia.**

TWITCHY EARS

Blink. Blink. Fidget. Fidget. Some people develop a nervous twitch. And so do some cats! A nervous cat might develop twitchy ears. Maybe a new cat has arrived in his neighbourhood and they don't get along. Or perhaps his family moved, forcing him to change territories.

But stress doesn't have to be dramatic and long-term to start a kitty's ear-twitching. A strange noise might do it. Cats hear much better than humans do. Humans only hear sounds up to 20,000 hertz, which is a measurement of how high or low pitched a sound is. Dogs do better. They hear noises up to 40,000 hertz. But cats do the best! They pick up 60,000 hertz, which we call ultrasound, because we can't hear it.

This means that cats hear mouse squeaks and a whole lot of other high-pitched sounds that we can only guess at. A cat's ears might twitch, even when he's asleep, if he hears something that might indicate danger. He has to decide. Should he jump up and run, or is it safe to keep snoozing? That's enough to make anyone antsy.

You can help by cooing softly to reassure him. But if the twitching continues, or his ears fold back, walk away and leave him be. He could be getting angry, and you don't want to become the target! Check in with him later, when he's calmed down.

Scientists think that cats respond better to women because women have higher-pitched voices than men.

WHAT'S THAT NOISE? I'VE NEVER HEARD IT BEFORE.

EARS TURNED SIGEWAYS

Here comes trouble. That's the phrase to remember when you see a cat whose ears are turned so that the openings face backward or to the sides. Cats rotate their ears when they're angry. They do it to show that they're ready to fight. It may not come to that, of course. In the end, either he or his opponent may back down and slink away.

But suppose your cat is angry with you. Perhaps he enjoyed having you pet him at first, but now he wants you to stop. He tells you so by narrowing his eyes and swivelling his ears. If you are paying attention and recognize the signs, you can avoid being potentially scratched or bitten.

Turned ears don't always mean a cat is in a bad mood. Cats also swivel their ears to find out exactly where an intriguing sound is coming from. If necessary, they can even point each ear in a different direction. Then they analyze the data and go wherever their ears lead them. It's like having a never-fail, built-in GPS system. No wonder cats excel at finding mice skittering through tall grass, after dark.

Cats hear us call, and they recognize our voice. When they don't come, it's because they're ignoring us.

WHISKERS POINTING SIDEWAYS

Tigers have them. So do bobcats, leopards, and your own pet kitty. They're called whiskers, and they give cats an elegant appearance. Whiskers are stiff hairs about twice as thick as the hairs on a human's head. Most domestic cats have four rows of them on either side of their nose. They grow out of an area rich with blood vessels and nerve endings, and they are rooted three times deeper than a regular hair.

But whiskers do more than look sharp. They help cats find their way around, assist them in nabbing prey, and show how they're feeling. A cat can turn her whiskers every which way, as she can with her ears, and she can move the top two rows separately from the bottom two. If a cat feels happy, calm, or friendly, she points her whiskers out to the sides in a graceful, relaxed fan. She does the same thing when she's walking in the dark.

That's when whiskers really come in handy. They are so supersensitive that they detect the teensy breezes created every time air passes around a solid object. And they bend when they touch something. Then they relay info about these obstacles directly to the brain. It makes a great early warning system. Using whiskers and night vision, a cat could probably explore any dark, twisting, underground cave without bumping into things.

Bare-naked Sphynx cats don't have any whiskers.

Sphynx

I'M WARNING YOU— STAY OUT OF MY 'HOOD.

DR. GARY'S VET TIPS

MANY CATS are very fussy about the shape of their food dish. They don't like having their supersensitive whiskers hitting the sides of a bowl. You can make your cat happy by feeding him from a dish, whether round or flat, in which this won't happen. Most cats eat well out of a saucer.

WHISKERS POINTING BACKWARD

Uh-oh. Your cat has pulled his whiskers back so they lie flat against his face. Pulled back whiskers are a sure sign of aggression or fear. If your kitty flattens his when he's sitting on your lap, something has scared him. Maybe he's heard a strange noise or another cat has entered the room. Whatever the reason, he wants to escape. So let him go!

Female cats and neutered males generally steer clear of each other when they can. Tomcats tell a different story. Tomcats are unneutered males. Their name comes from an old book called *The Life and Adventures of a Cat*. Published in England in 1760, it starred a feline called "Tom the Cat".

The book was such a hit that "tomcat" quickly became a household word.

Today, so many pets are neutered that most tomcats are strays or feral. Feral cats are born in the wild and have never had any human contact. Strays are former pets that got lost or abandoned. But all toms—whether feral, stray, or family pets that are allowed outdoors—have huge territories. Having to defend these territories (which can be ten times bigger than those of females) means that tomcats treat other males as rivals, not friends.

And when two of them meet, fur flies. Pulling back their whiskers helps protect them during fights.

Persian cats have such flat faces that they can't move their whiskers at all.

Persian

OH, BOY! THIS IS GOING TO BE GOOD!

DR. GARY'S VET TIPS

CAT WHISKERS come in different lengths. They vary by cat and by breed. Maine coon cats have large and long whiskers, probably to match their large bodies. American wirehairs have short and curly ones. But it isn't true that a cat's whole body will fit through any opening his whiskers fit through. Cats, especially kittens, get stuck all the time. And many adult cats are overweight. Their whiskers don't grow longer just because their appetite increases.

WHISKERS POINTING FORWARD

No question about it. This cat is excited. Either he's angry or he's after something. Just look at his low, tense body and forward-pointing whiskers. A cat searching for prey in the dark fans out his whiskers and sweeps them along in front of him. His whiskers keep him from banging into things and allow him to approach in silence. That way he can sneak up on birds and rodents and mount a surprise attack.

Whiskers also act like a handheld treasure finder, except that they "beep" when they find mice, not metal. They are so sensitive they can pick up the tiny vibrations made by a mouse rustling in the grass and point the cat directly toward it.

When the cat's cheek whiskers brush against a mouse, they send a signal to the cat's brain: Pounce here, now! If all goes well, the cat will attack, deliver a killing bite, and savor his catch. But sometimes a bite misses its mark, and the prey survives. When that happens, a cat could end up with a live rat dangling from his mouth. Then the rat could turn on the cat and injure him badly. So whiskers come into play again. A cat curls them around his catch like hands around a ball, and they warn him of any movement. If they sense any, the excitement begins again.

Kittens are born **blind and deaf** but with the touch sensors on their **whiskers** already working.

WHAT IS THIS CaT SAYING?

The Scenario

Sabrina, a 17-year-old blind cat got lost. Her frantic owner, Maria Elena Colomer, spent nearly a month driving around her South Florida, U.S.A., neighbourhood looking for her. One day, she passed Eida Hernandez, who was feeding some strays. Colomer asked her if she had seen her lost kitty. Hernandez had not, but she remembered the crying woman who drove a silver car.

Weeks later, a teenager found an old, skinny, blind cat wandering the streets. She called the police, who took the cat to Alton Road Animal Hospital. Meanwhile, the Spanish-speaking Hernandez teamed up with an English-speaking Alton Road Hospital volunteer to trap and rescue some wild kittens. Despite the language barrier, the two women managed to compare notes on stray cats they had helped.

When the second woman mentioned the blind cat at the veterinary hospital, Hernandez's face lit up. That must be the cat the sad lady had lost!

By now, four months had passed. The volunteers called the police, and an animal services officer scoured the neighbourhood until she found a silver car. Sure enough, it belonged to Colomer. Today, thanks to an army of cat lovers, Sabrina is safely back home.

You Be the Expert

Do blind cats make good pets? Can they live fulfilling lives? How do you think Sabrina managed to survive for so long on her own?

No one wants a cat to be blind, and it's a shame. But blind cats make wonderful pets. They have other senses that can very much make up for their loss of sight—whiskers, keen hearing, and a strong sense of smell. While she was lost, Sabrina could smell out drinking water, but she couldn't do much hunting because of her old age. She probably survived because some kind-hearted person put out food for her.

Supporting a Blind Cat

For safety's sake, cats that lose their vision must be kept indoors. Beyond that, their number one need is familiarity. So keep their food dishes and litter box in the same places, and don't keep moving the furniture willy-nilly. Otherwise, live normally. A blind cat will adjust.

That said, you can't just shut her inside and let her vegetate. She needs playtime for exercise and to keep her mind sharp. Avoid activities that rely strictly on eyesight, like chasing a rope toy or a laser pointer. Laser pointers can be frustrating even for sighted cats! But blind cats love squeaky toys, nibbling grass, rolling in catnip (if they're sensitive to it), cat trees, and scratching posts. Above all, enjoy your kitty, and she will enjoy her life with you.

HERE, KITTY, KITTY

Teaching your cat to "come"

Cats can hear five times better than you. So yours may already come when she hears the can opener turning or kibble hitting her dish. Here's how to get her to come when you call.

 Since cats are meat-eaters, take some leftover ham or chicken, your hungry kitty, and your clicker into a quiet room.

 Hold the clicker in one hand and some meat in the other. Waggle the meat under your cat's nose. Then hold it out to her. When she touches her nose to it, click and let her eat it. Remember, timing is everything. You must click at the exact moment your cat does what you want.

 Repeat several times, but keep moving back a little. Say your cat's name and the word, "come". Again, when her nose touches the food, click and give it to her.

 Feed your kitty like this every day for a week, and soon the sound of your voice will bring her running.

Abyssinian

TeLLING TAiLS

FOR TEN MILLION YEARS, cats lived solitary lives, hunting and competing for food. They had no need to "talk". But 10,000 years ago, things changed. Humans stopped living as hunters and gatherers and started growing grain. Their grain stockpiles attracted mice, and those mice attracted cats. Soon many cats hung out in the same places. To get along without clawing each other to bits, these loner cats suddenly needed to communicate. But they didn't know how!

Cats have learned a lot since then. They have evolved several signals to tell each other (and us) what they're thinking and feeling. Many of these signals involve their tails.

A cat's tail has as many as 28 bones, and it makes up one-third of its spine. Nature designed it as a counterweight to help cats leap, turn corners when running fast, and balance when walking out on skinny tree branches.

But today, the tail of a cat also serves as a barometer of kitty moods. So it's good to know the various feline tail positions. Then you won't misunderstand.

the FLUFFED-OUT TAIL

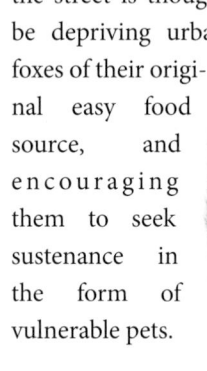

Confronted with a mean dog or a rival cat, what's a kitty to do? If she turns tail and runs, the other animal will chase her. If she tries to defend herself, she might end up in a brutal fight. A safer solution is to stand her ground and try to scare off the threat. But how? Instinct takes over. Adrenaline surges through the frightened cat's body and makes her hair stand on end. Her tail puffs out like a bottle brush, and she holds it away from her body. The pose is mostly bluff and, in a kitten, looks more cute than threatening. But all cats do it, hoping to look big and scary... With luck, she'll look so big and scary that whatever is threatening her will run away.

Mean dogs and other cats aren't the only dangers kitties face. In many big cities like Edinburgh and London, foxes can pose a serious risk. Urban foxes often struggle to find enough food to eat in the city, and as a result, they are having to resort to other options—preying on domestic cats. People have reported seeing their cats being attacked by foxes, resulting in hefty vet bills for stitches and antibiotics. Some owners have even had to witness their cats being killed by foxes. Using plastic wheelie bins to dispose of rubbish rather than bin bags left in the street is thought to be depriving urban foxes of their original easy food source, and encouraging them to seek sustenance in the form of vulnerable pets.

Sydney, Australia, has a
cat curfew.
To protect ringtail possums
and other native wildlife,
cats must stay inside
from dusk to dawn.

DON'T MESS WITH ME!
I'M BIGGER THAN YOU.

the WAGGING TAIL

You might think a wagging tail means a cat is being friendly. It doesn't! Just like with dogs, different wags mean different things. But with cats, it gets especially confusing. Cats' communication signals are less developed than those of dogs, making their tail wags harder to interpret.

Even the experts don't always agree. One says that an angry cat waves his tail slowly. Another insists that a slowly swishing tail means a mouse, toy, or another cat has captured your cat's attention. Still a third believes a wagging tail is a sign of indecision. Suppose your cat asked to go out. You opened the door, but now he just stands there wagging his tail.

That can be exasperating! But maybe he smells the neighbour's cat or hears a dog barking. Is going out too dangerous? His tail won't stop wagging until he makes up his mind.

So where does this leave you? First, spend time watching your own cat and getting to know him as an individual. Each cat has his own personality and his own way of behaving. Then look at the whole cat, including his eyes, ears, body, whiskers, and tail. Put it all together and you should get an idea of what he's thinking.

Always play it safe. If you're stroking your cat when his tail starts moving, stop! Otherwise he might claw *you*.

Herodotus,
an ancient Greek historian, called cats *ailuroi*, which means "tail wavers".

TO GO OUT
OR NOT TO
GO OUT.
THAT IS THE
QUESTION.

DR. GARY'S VET TIPS

LIKE WITH dogs, almost everything you ever wanted to know about your cat is being told by his tail. But cats' tails and dogs' tails speak very different languages. When a dog holds his tail straight up, he's alert, or possibly angry. A cat does that when she's feeling friendly. A happy dog wags his tail broadly. A tail-wagging cat could be mad—and so on. No wonder cats and dogs sometimes misunderstand each other. If we aren't careful, we humans can easily get confused, too.

Siamese

the TWITCHING TAIL

What's up with a cat that twitches her tail? She's lying somewhere all comfy-cozy, but the tip of her tail is jerking back and forth like the pendulum on an old-fashioned clock. The answer is that she feels uneasy. She may be curious, annoyed, or frustrated. Whatever emotion she is experiencing keeps her alert. But it isn't strong enough to make her get up and take action … yet.

If her whole tail is twitching, however, check out her face. If her ears are back, her eyes wide and staring, and her body looks tense, watch out! She's either angry or getting ready to pounce. Stalking cats often hold their tails low and stiff. They try to remain completely motionless, but their tail starts twitching and gives them away. This is called a hunting twitch. To see it, drag a piece of yarn across the floor and in and out around the chairs. Your kitty will crouch down and freeze, but then her tail will start jerking. That twitch comes from excitement. It's a release of the energy built up by her effort to stay still.

Cats' tails also quiver, but there's a big difference between quivering and twitching. A quivering tail doesn't jerk; it vibrates. Any cat, whether male or female, that backs up against an object and lifts a quivering tail is neither hunting nor curious. That cat is going to spray a shot of pee!

Most cats catch more mice than birds. That's partly because birds can spot a cat's tail twitching from up above.

the THRASHING TAIL

Thump! Thump! Swish! Swish! Your cat is staring out the window either pounding his tail on the sill or whipping it madly back and forth. With dogs this would be a sign of happy excitement. Not so with cats.

A tail-thumping cat is excited, all right, but not in a good way. His excitement is wrapped up in frustration and emotional upset. He's probably watching birds through the glass that he knows he can't reach. Or he might have his eye on a trespassing cat prowling around outside, in his territory. The faster your cat's tail moves and the more forward he points his ears, the greater his turmoil.

The best thing you can do is stay away from a cat that is in such a state. Don't try to pick him up, and if you're already holding him, let him go. It doesn't matter how sweet and loving your kitty normally is. If he can't direct his anger and frustration where it really belongs, he might turn it on you.

One breed of cat, called the Manx, doesn't have a tail to thrash. That makes it much harder to tell if they are feeling cross. Luckily, these glossy-coated beauties are exceptionally calm by nature.

Stewie, a **Maine coon** cat, holds the world record for the longest tail on a pet cat, at **16.3 inches (41.4 cm) long.**

Bengal

HI, THERE.
I COME IN
PEACE.

DR. GARY'S VET TIPS

A LITTLE house cat has more bones in her body than you or I have in ours. While adult humans have only 206, a cat can have as many as 245. It depends on how many toes she has and the number of bones in her tail. Like those of a dog, a cat's tail bones are part of her spine. The difference is that a cat's backbones are very loosely connected, which makes a cat supremely flexible. But that also makes her bones easily dislocated. So never pull a cat's (or any animal's) tail or pick up a cat by her tail.

the STRAIGHT-UP TAIL

Humans shake hands. Cats hold up their tails. When your kitty walks toward you with her tail up, she's happy to see you. If the tip is bent or twitching, that's even better. She clearly adores you and wants to snuggle or body rub.

But guess what! This tail position is a new behaviour. Our lovable pets' wildcat ancestors didn't do it. Only their kittens did, when greeting their mothers. It's a mystery why.

Adult cats first adopted the habit after humans began farming. That's when cats moved into colonies near humans, where there were plenty of mice. To show each other they wanted to get along, some lifted their tails. Over 10,000 years, the signal evolved. Today, all cats know it.

To be sure of its meaning, scientist John Bradshaw cut life-size cat silhouettes out of black paper. Some had an upright tail and some had a horizontal one. He taped these shapes to the walls inside houses where pet cats lived. Sure enough, the cats walked right up and sniffed the high tails. But they backed away from the others.

What we still don't know is if cats came up with this signal to make peace with each other first and then used it with us, or the other way around. But it works with both, and it's adorable.

A group of kittens is called a **kindle.**
A group of adult cats is called a **clowder.**

Tokinese

the WRAPPED-AROUND TAIL

It's a classic cat posture. A sleek-looking feline sits on her haunches, like an Egyptian cat statue. Her tail winds around her feet. Or she lies on her stomach with her paws tucked under and her tail wrapped around her body. "Isn't that just like a cat?" we say. "So snooty and standoffish."

But we misunderstand. A cat with a wrapped-around tail is like a person with his arms crossed in front of his chest. Both feel wary and unsure of themselves. Probably without even realizing it, they're each using body parts to create a sort of shield. It's a polite way of telling other people or approaching cats to keep their distance.

If you see two unrelated cats stationed in the same place, chances are they won't just have wrapped-around tails. They'll also have their backs turned to each other. And there they will stay, as still as statues. Neither one dares to move for fear the other will notice and attack.

Trouble is, relaxed cats sometimes wrap their tails. So how can you tell if a cat is calm or uneasy? It's simple. Is his body tense? Is there another cat around? Are his ears pricked forward or turned? Then the message is, "Stay away." But if he's alone, his eyes are closed, and his ears relaxed, *shhh.* It's naptime.

In 1888, an **Egyptian farmer** accidentally discovered a huge, single grave containing 300,000 mummified cats.

Snowshoe

the CURVED-UPWARD TAIL

Kittens love to play rough. They pounce. They bite. They wrestle and roll around—all in good fun. But the older kittens get, the rougher they play. Sometimes, one kitten scratches or bites the other too hard. When that happens, the offending kitten will get a relaxed look on his face, called a "play face". That reassures the kitty that got hurt that this is just a game and not a fight.

But that doesn't always work. Sometimes the kitten that got bitten or scratched simply wants to quit playing. He "says" he has had enough by arching his back, curling his tail upward, and jumping straight up into the air.

Kittens that are born an "only child" or taken away from their mother too soon often play too rough. If an "only kitten" is put in with other kittens, they will usually refuse to play with him at all. Maybe a lack of communication is part of the reason why. Perhaps the other kittens won't play because the "only" kitten doesn't understand the "secret" sign that means they want to stop.

This funny-looking signal is only used by kittens, but only kittens need it. An adult cat might occasionally play with a kitten, but adults don't play with other adults. They only play with toys. That means that adult cats can play as rough as they want, and nobody gets hurt.

Kittens must be held and stroked every day between the ages of two and eight weeks, or they will remain forever wild.

Siamese

A cat that **wraps her tail**
around your leg
is showing **affection.**

Singapura

WE'RE
TOTALLY BFFs.

TWINING TAILS

Ahh. The sweet smell of home. This really matters to cats. It's how they identify family members, friends, and the objects they live with. They want everything and everyone to smell exactly the same.

We can't even smell it, but without that familiar "family odour", cats feel anxious and insecure. Because it's so important, they frequently go around the house trying to replenish it. They rub the scent glands in their chin, their cheeks, the corners of their mouth, their forehead, and along their tail on everything they can reach.

Some cats have a special way of saying "hi" when one cat greets a related cat that already shares his family odour. They hold their tails up and entwine them. Then they walk along "holding tails". Many scientists think cats do this just because it feels good, and making each other feel good cements their bond. Two closely bonded cats will find it easier to live together and have much fewer squabbles. Since cats aren't good at making friends anyway, this really helps.

If these scientists are right, then tail twining is like you walking arm in arm with a good friend. It brings the cats closer and shows the world that they are best buds. All of which makes tail twining a pretty important gesture.

Oriental shorthair

DR. GARY'S VET TIPS

IF YOU have more than one cat, and one cat needs to go to the vet, try to bring them all along. What's that you're saying? "No way! It's hard enough just bringing one." That's true. It can be a real pain loading multiple cats into their carriers. But if you have them clicker trained to enter on command (see Training Tips, p. 107) you can do it. And it's worth it. Many cat fights occur after one cat has been to the vet, because that cat has lost his "family odour" and smells different when he returns. If they all go, and the vet pets all of them, then they'll all smell the same when you take them back home.

WHAT IS THIS CaT SAYING?

The Scenario

Blackie the kitten was wild. He belonged to a cat colony—a large group of homeless cats that lived together on the streets. Because Blackie was born outdoors and never had any contact with humans, he was a feral cat. His mother raised Blackie and his two sisters by feeding them milk from her body. Later, she hunted mice and rats for them to eat.

Blackie survived his first winter, but seemed unhealthy in the spring. He slept a lot, ate little, and never grew to normal size. One day, Blackie left the colony and moved onto the front porch of a nearby house, where he slept curled up on the doormat. If a person approached, Blackie jumped up and ran away. But whenever one of his sisters came, he rubbed noses with her. Sometimes the two walked side by side with their tails entwined—a true sign of kitty friendship.

You Be the Expert

Why did Blackie leave his colony? How come cats can live peaceably together outside, but not indoors?

Cats are predators that compete with each other for food. But they also fall prey to bigger animals, like foxes. So they protect themselves by hiding when they're sick. Blackie most likely left his colony to go into hiding because he didn't feel well enough to compete. Sleeping on the porch gave him a roof over his head and something soft to lie on. He stayed because the homeowner put out food for him.

Cats are practical. Even though individuals struggle to get along with each other, if there's enough food

available, they sometimes learn to coexist. That's why cat colonies often spring up in large, open places near barns, bins, and cat sanctuaries. Colonies consist of several small groups of mothers, sisters, and kittens. Occasionally a tom shows up. They don't fight because there's room enough for each cat to have its own space.

How to Help Feral Cats

All around the world, volunteer caretakers look out for homeless cats. Nonprofit organizations help limit their numbers by sponsoring Trap, Neuter, and Return (TNR) programs. Trained adults capture wild cats, get them fixed so they can't have kittens, and return them to their colonies.

Perhaps the best place to be a homeless cat is Rome, Italy. In 1991 Italy passed a no-kill law that gives feral cats the right to stay wherever they're born. Today, about 300,000 cats live in 2,000 cat colonies located in cave-like areas underneath the city streets. Kindhearted volunteers, called the *gattare*, feed and care for them.

You can help by getting your own pets neutered and donating to the cause.

JUMPING FROM CHAIR TO CHAIR

Showcase your kitty's athletic ability.

 Shove two kitchen chairs together so they're facing each other. Put your cat on one of them. With him watching, set a tasty treat in the middle of the second chair.

 Use your fingers to tap the chair next to the treat. He should walk over and eat it.

 Put another treat on the first chair. Tap next to it and say, "come over".

 Repeat these steps several times, in both directions.

 While kitty is eating a treat, pull the chairs a few inches apart.

 Put a treat on the empty chair, tap it, and say, "come over". Repeat. At each training session, move the chairs a little farther apart.

 Most house (or pet) cats like working for food. They're designed to hunt, after all, and can get bored. Training your cat lets him use his brain and gives him something interesting to do. Eventually, you can try having him jump through a hoop on his way across.

CaT CHaT

HAS YOUR KITTY "TOLD" YOU lately that she loves you? Has she "asked" to eat or demanded to go outside? Chances are the answer is yes. Pet cats are quite vocal around their owners. The funny thing is that feral cats live silent lives. A feral cat might raise his tail to say "hi" to another cat and then miaow if the other cat ignores him. And all cats make a racket when fighting. But otherwise, feral cats rarely speak.

This is especially odd considering that pet kittens begin sounding off just days after birth. By three months of age, they will have picked up a wide range of sounds they'll use the rest of their lives. They learn so many chitters, hisses, and miaows that an adult cat's "playlist" includes 30 to 100 different selections. Dogs have fewer than 20.

To make it easier, experts divide cat sounds into three categories: murmurs, miaows, and high-intensity sounds. Murmurs are soft sounds, like purrs. Everyone knows a miaow when they hear it. High-intensity sounds include snarls, growls, and noises made under stress. Certainly, kitty lingo can be tricky for humans to translate. But it's worth trying, because understanding even a little bit will make life happier for you and your cat.

CHATTERING

The sun is shining. Blue jays, sparrows, and robins are flitting around in your garden. Inside the house, your cat sits staring out the window. His ears are perked forward. His tail swishes, and his teeth are chattering.

Chattering teeth? This high-intensity sound is produced under stress. It sounds weird, but your kitty is frustrated. He's clacking his teeth the way he would if he could pounce through the glass and snatch one of those birds by the neck. Just watching excites him at first. It would be like you watching waiters heap a banquet table with pizzas, chips, and banana splits. Your mouth might even water. But then, suppose all that yummy-ness was off limits. You couldn't reach it!

Well, neither can an indoor cat.

Some people keep their cats inside for safety reasons. But others do it because of a recent research study. This highly controversial study blames cats for killing billions of birds a year and potentially making some species go extinct. More research needs to be done. But if this concerns you, understand that well-fed pets often pounce halfheartedly and go away empty-pawed. Loss of habitat may be a bigger threat to the birds. So some experts believe it's better to help the birds than to lock up the cats. Plant berry bushes or hang a bird feeder where cats can't reach. That will help keep birds safely up off the ground, where cats can't catch them.

A cat
in Russia barks
like a dog.

JUST OPEN THIS WINDOW AND LET ME AT 'EM.

DR. GARY'S VET TIPS

CATS ARE born hunters and stalkers. There's no question that they kill birds and other wildlife. But there is a huge question over how many they kill. If the idea of this worries you, keep your cat inside—but give her plenty to do. If you must let her out, put a collar on her and hang a lightweight warning bell on it so that birds and rabbits will hear her coming. Check the collar regularly to see that it isn't too tight, and be sure to use a "break-away" style. A break-away collar will pop open if your cat snags it on a bush. Otherwise, it could be dangerous and strangle her if it gets caught on a branch outside.

HISSING and SPITTING

Cats and snakes. Mammal versus reptile. One cuddles; the other slithers. These two creatures couldn't possibly have anything in common, could they? Surprisingly, they do. They are alike in two important ways.

First of all, they sometimes sound alike. Cats and snakes both hiss when they're trying to defend themselves. A cat waits until her enemy gets close. Then she tries to scare it off by opening her mouth halfway and blowing out a sudden, big blast of air. Sometimes she also spits. It's an effective technique. Even much bigger animals will startle and jump back. And all cats can do it, right down to newborn kittens. So forget the bad things you've heard about throwing a hissy fit. Sometimes it can be a lifesaver.

The other trait shared by cats and snakes is that both have a strange structure in the roof of their mouth called a Jacobson's organ. The Jacobson's organ lets a cat taste the air as well as smell it! When she's using it, she'll make a funny face. No sound comes out, but she opens her mouth and pulls back her upper lip to show her teeth. She'll stay like this for several seconds, taking everything in. Then she uses the clues she collects to track down other cats or locate prey from a distance.

Besides cats and snakes, opossums and **baby hedgehogs** also hiss when threatened.

Angora

WAKE UP, WAKE UP, YOU LAZY LUGS! TIME'S A WASTIN'.

YOWLING

Better cover your ears. Of the dozens of sounds cats make, yowling is the loudest. And the most annoying! Cats yowl when they're angry. They yowl when they're confused, disoriented, or in pain. And they really wail when one cat enters another cat's territory or two tomcats squabble over mates. Fighting cats raise their voices higher and higher, in an ear-splitting duet called caterwauling, until one of them attacks.

Cats are most active after dark, because that's when they hunt. So most "concerts" take place at night. Many happen out-of-doors, on the garden fences of cartoon fame. But some cats sound off inside. Elderly cats that don't feel well or whose minds aren't sharp might wail when they're alone and the house is quiet.

Healthy cats do it for attention. Say it's 3:00 a.m. You're sound asleep, when *Aiiiieeeee!* You groan. You yell. You cover your head with your pillow. Finally, in desperation, you get up and pour kibble in a dish. Maybe that will shut him up. It does. But your quick-learning feline does it again every night from then on, because he knows it works.

The only way to tell why your cat carries on is to consider the context. Look at when and where he makes the noise. If you're not sure what's wrong, take him to the vet.

No two cats
sound alike.
Each cat, like each person,
has a voice of
his or her own.

Maine Coon

DR. GARY'S VET TIPS

A CAT can make at least 16 different miaows. If you want to learn their meanings, why not record them? Keep a small battery-powered digital recorder or a smartphone handy. Each time your cat sounds off, record her miaow along with a description of where she is, what she's doing, and what she wants. Then you can play the recordings back until you have them memorized. Pretty soon, you'll be fluent in cat talk.

MIAOWING

A kitty's miaow is the most recognizable cat sound we know. But here's something you may not know: Cats hardly ever miaow to each other. They only miaow to their people. Being clever little animals, cats quickly realize that we humans are not very observant, at least when it comes to them. Either we don't notice their moving tails and changing ear positions, or we ignore them. But we do react to noise.

So cats build on that. When kittens are eight to ten weeks old, they begin trying out a variety of sounds on their owners. Whichever ones get them what they want, they use again and again. Many cats miaow to say "hello".

But miaows can mean anything. Not surprisingly, most of them are requests or complaints. Pet cats "say" things like "Feed me," "Stroke me," "What took you so long?" and "Let me out."

Pay close attention to your own kitty. Listen to his sounds and watch his behaviour. Before long, you'll begin to associate certain sounds with specific actions and places. Maybe he makes one miaow when he's sitting by a closed door and a different one when he's standing by his empty dish. Figuring them out can be fun. Over time, you both will develop your own private "language", which is like a secret code. Neither other people nor other cats will understand it.

The average cat miaows **six times** a day.

Kurilian bobtail

PURRING

Most of us find a kitty's purr *mew*-sic to our ears. It relaxes us when we're nervous and cheers us up when we're sad. That's certainly how the residents of a Madrid, Iowa, U.S.A., nursing home feel. They consider the purrs of a calico cat named Willow so soothing that they made her their official "comfort cat".

Few people realize that purring doesn't always mean a cat is content. Cats do purr when they're happy. But their "motors" also rumble when they're sick, injured, or feeling stressed. Scientists now believe purring is a request for company. A cat could feel great or he could need a friend to hold his hand, er, paw. It's possible that purring releases endorphins, feel-good chemicals in a cat's brain. If so, then it's as comforting for him as it is for us.

Experts recently discovered two more things: The purring sound comes from vibrating muscles in a cat's voice box. And there are two kinds of purrs. There is the normal, "nice" purr and the demanding, "feed me" purr. Some cats, but not all, mix a slightly whiny cry into their purr so that it sounds like a human baby crying. This feed me purr makes people abandon their own breakfast to feed their cat first. This is, of course, exactly what Her Furry Highness expects.

Domestic cats can
purr and miaow
at the same time.

WHAT IS THIS CaT SAYING?

The Scenario

Max, a handsome gray tabby, never stops "talking". Adopted from an animal shelter as a kitten, he received lots of attention. His owners stroked and cuddled him. Every day, Max would jump onto one of their laps with a soft ball in his mouth. They'd toss it, and he would play fetch.

Then his owners adopted a dog, moved to a bigger house, and had a baby. Max's quiet domain now hums with activity. And Max only adds to the noise. Never at a loss for words, he raises his tail, rubs against his people, and miaows contentedly. When mother and baby play on the floor, Max miaows and paces back and forth between them. He even miaows in the middle of the night, when everyone is trying to sleep.

The family adores Max, but his non-stop talking is getting on their nerves.

You Be the Expert

Why is Max such a loudmouth? How can the family make him stop so they can enjoy some peace and quiet?

Max obviously wants attention. And what better time to get it than at 2:00 a.m., when everyone else is asleep and the house is dark? It all started one night when he miaowed so loudly that he woke everyone up. Desperate for some shut-eye, his owner stumbled to the kitchen and threw some food in his dish. One time! That's all it took to create a furry monster.

The moral is to never let this happen in the first place. Cats are so amazingly persistent. Think how they'll wait by a mouse hole for hours and hours. Once a cat has gotten what he wants, he'll keep it up. The best thing you can do is stop "rewarding" his bad behaviour. Granted, this is hard. You'll probably need ear plugs to outlast your cat.

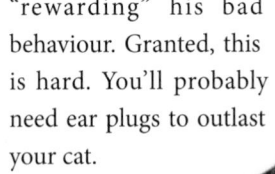

Helping Your Cat Entertain Himself

If Max was a Siamese, there wouldn't be much his owners could do. Constant talking is a trait with all Siamese cats. And if Max was an outdoor kitty, his owners wouldn't have this problem. Outdoor cats hunt and roam all day and come in at night ready to sleep.

But Max is an indoor cat, and he's easily bored. So now his owners make an effort to play fetch with him again, like they did before the baby came and the dog arrived. They also set out open boxes and paper bags for him to hide inside. To deaden the noise, they made Max a cozy bed on a high shelf in their utility room—the room farthest away from their bedroom. They put food, water, and a litter box in there, and shut the door on him at night.

Is he "speechless" now? Hardly. But he's quieter than before.

FOR SAFETY'S SAKE

Getting your cat to go into his carrier.

 Leave your cat's carrier open and sitting in the living room. Then it won't seem strange and scary. Click and reward your kitty whenever he walks toward it. Use really yummy treats.

 Once he's doing that, click and treat only when he pokes his head inside.

 Now wait until he steps inside to click and treat. Be patient. Resist the urge to put him in yourself.

 Start holding off on the treats for three or four seconds. Then click and reward him for staying inside the carrier.

 Try closing the door on him. If he stays calm, click and open the door. Give him a treat.

 Finally, point to the carrier and say, "inside". If kitty obeys, click and treat. Practise daily for five minutes at a time. And keep at it. Mastering this could take weeks, but it will turn an often stressful procedure into a calm experience for both you and your cat.

British shorthair

TROUBLE TaLK

PEOPLE FORGET THAT CATS are miniature tigers. Watch a nature show on TV, and you'll see tigers raking their nails, spraying urine, and ambushing elk. But when our beloved kitties shred the curtains, pee on the carpet, or leave dead mice on our pillow, we humans take offense. Behavioural problems are the second most common reason for people surrendering their cats to shelters (health and personal problems rank first). Since shelters euthanize up to two million cats each year because they are unable to find them all forever homes, correcting bad cat behaviour actually saves lives. And it isn't as difficult as it may seem.

Read on to explore some common troubling cat behaviours. Remember, the first step is to not take it personally. Understand that your cat isn't trying to hurt you. Or seeking revenge. He's just doing what comes naturally.

BITING

Most cats bite out of fear. They'd rather run away, but they feel cornered and can't. So they lash out. But fear isn't always the cause. Some cats seem to bite "out of the blue", for no reason at all. Kitty might be lying on your lap purring as you stroke her back. Then, *Yow!* She sinks her teeth into your wrist. This hurts your wrist and your feelings.

Don't worry. Your cat loves you. She's just overly sensitive, like extremely ticklish people. The stroking may feel good at first, but she can only stand so much. Now she wants you to stop!

Whatever her problem is, cat bites can be serious. Germs from a cat's mouth can enter the wound and cause infection. There's even a risk of rabies, if the cat hasn't been vaccinated.

Protect yourself by washing all bites or scratches with soap and water. And if the bite breaks the skin, go to the doctor. Here are some tips for preventing bites in the first place:

- Only an adult wearing gloves or a trained medical professional should handle an injured cat.

- Never interfere when cats are fighting.

- Be alert for feline warning signals—flattened ears, a thrashing tail, tense muscles, hissing, or spitting.

- Whenever possible, give cats an escape route.

- If your cat can't handle being stroked, try to understand. Accept and love her the way she is.

Cats have 30 teeth, 4 of which are extra long and specially designed to catch and kill prey.

I'VE HAD ENOUGH. STOP STROKING ME NOW!

DR. GARY'S VET TIPS

CATS LIKE being stroked where their scent glands are located—base of the chin, ears, and tail, and on their cheeks. Touching a cat in these places releases his scent and makes him content. Begin by touching a cat's nose with your finger, so he can smell you. Then rub or scratch the top of his head between his ears. Next, move the palm of your hand from his head to his tail, in one long motion. Don't touch his tummy. And be aware that a cat that jumps onto your lap doesn't always want to be stroked. He may just want to lie where it's warm.

SPRAYING

Cats sometimes squirt urine to leave "Smell-it" notes for other felines. This is different than going to the bathroom and is called spraying. You can tell which is which by checking the wet spot. If it's on the floor, your cat had to go and didn't use his box. If it's against a vertical surface, like a fence or door, he's marking his territory.

Scent-marking takes place both indoors and out. Cats do it when they're worried about a rival, whether a roaming stray or a new pet in the house. The spraying cat comforts himself with the familiar smell of his own pee and hopes to warn the intruder to stay away.

One in ten cats, both males and females, sprays. But unneutered males do it the most. Getting them neutered often solves the problem.

When it doesn't, you need to take stronger measures, or the spraying will get worse. First, clean the spot using warm water and an enzyme-based laundry detergent. Then use a squirt bottle to spray rubbing alcohol on the site. Wait 24 hours. Cover the site with aluminium foil, and set your cat's food dish on top. Most cats won't spray where they eat.

But you aren't done yet. You also must find and remove the cause of the stress. Only then will you eliminate the problem.

Every cat has its own individual scent, which is as unique as a human's fingerprint.

Persian

PEE-YEW! DO THEY REALLY EXPECT ME TO GO IN THAT?

DR. GARY'S VET TIPS

FAT CATS and older cats often suffer from constipation. Their stools are small and hard and painful to pass. Feeding cats canned food, instead of dry, helps because of its higher water content. So does dieting. Fat cats really need to lose weight!

REFUSING TO USE THE LITTER BOX

Mama cats and nature house-train kittens. In the wild, cats bury their poo to hide it from other animals. So, for a pet to deny that instinct and go where she can't cover it up, instead of in her litter box, means she is very upset. Figuring out why takes work. But you need to do it, and soon. Studies show that many people hate cleaning up cat messes so much that they get rid of their cat.

This is sad, because the problem can be fixed. Usually the problem is anxiety, but sometimes it's medical, and you may need to head to the vet. If he's healthy, then check his box. Is it clean? Some cats are super fussy. They want the litter changed at least every two weeks and the poo scooped every day—maybe to reduce the odour. Wash the box when you change the litter, using washing up liquid. Avoid bleach or anything strong-smelling, and steer clear of perfumed litter, too. Remember, a feline's nose is 100 times more sensitive than ours.

Then, make sure the box is big enough. Fill it with small-grained clumping litter, which most cats prefer, and place it in an easy-to-reach, out-of-the-way spot. Cats are like humans: They value their privacy. If you have more than one cat, give them each their own box. Finally, feed your cat in a separate spot. No one likes eating in the bathroom. Do all this, and your cat should be a happy litter-box user.

A cat in Brooklyn, New York, is **best friends** with an iguana.

SCRATCHING the FURNITURE

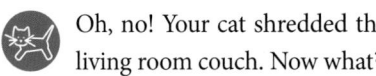 Oh, no! Your cat shredded the living room couch. Now what?

First, understand that cats don't mean to destroy things; they just need to scratch. Scratching exercises their muscles, relieves stress, and conditions their claws. It also transfers smell from the scent glands between their toes to whatever they scratch. These smells warn other cats to stay away and make your pet feel more at home. To cats, scratching is as natural as breathing.

So you can't make a cat stop. But you can teach him to scratch someplace else. The trick is to make whatever he's scratching unappealing. Shops sell double-sided tape that you can attach directly to furniture or put on sheets of cardboard. If you put it on cardboard, then you can lift the cardboard off when you want to sit. It works because cats hate sticky paws. Of course, you have to give your kitty an irresistible scratching post to use instead.

Keeping your cat's nails trimmed also helps. Every four weeks, take him to a professional groomer or do it yourself. To learn how, talk to your groomer or vet and watch videos. The helpful YouTube video, "How to Trim Your Cat's Claws", created by a vet, can be found at tinyurl.com/howtospeak cattrim.

It's good to do this anyway, especially if your cat likes to lie on your lap moving his claws in and out. Clipping his nails protects the furniture and you!

Most cats have 18 toes, but one cat in Canada has 28.

HOW DO YOU LIKE MY PAWSICURE?

Chartreux

DR. GARY'S VET TIPS

DECLAWING IS an unnecessary surgery on a cat's toes to prevent him from scratching. It's very painful and can lead to chronic pain, arthritis, and ligament damage. Not to mention behaviour problems! While declawing does protect the furniture, it's unnatural and is actually illegal in many places, like Europe. "Soft Paws" are a great alternative. These are acrylic caps glued to a cat's nails. They come in many fun colours and look cool. But just make sure to keep doing it, because the caps fall off when the nails grow out.

BULLYING

You probably know one—a bully who delights in tormenting other people. Well, bully cats act just as bad, sometimes terrifying their victims into living under the bed. And well-meaning humans are often to blame! We love cats so much that we force unrelated felines to live together, even though cats think other cats just want to steal their territory.

You have a bully on your hands if you find tipped over plants, tufts of hair, blood on the floor, or a cat with bitten ears. Behavioural signs include spraying, glaring contests, or a cat that stops eating, grooming, or using the litter box.

First, protect the victim. Cover the bully's nails with acrylic caps and attach a warning bell to his collar. Make sure each cat has its own facilities and space. Then give the victim an escape hatch. Install a cat door leading to a cupboard or other safe place. Choose a door that ties into the microchip of the victim, so only she can use it. Or make a hidey-hole out of a cardboard box, with a door cut in one side. Clicker training helps, too. Cats love it. Teach the bully to high-five, give him rewards, and he might forget about saving his territory.

If nothing works, find a new home for the victim. Nobody, human or feline, should live in fear.

BEAT IT, PAL! YOU'RE NOT WELCOME HERE.

A cat's territory can be as large as
17 city blocks
or as small as a placemat.

HUNGER GAMES

Eww! Your well-fed cat catches a mouse. But rather than eat it, she flicks it into the air and bats it with her paws. Then she drops it and lets it try to run away before she pounces and grabs it again. It looks so cruel.

But the truth is that if your cat sees moving prey, she has no choice. Hungry or not, she is hard-wired to go after it. And once she catches it, she may be so excited that she keeps replaying the moment. It's much like the fisherman who practises "catch and release". He doesn't want to eat the fish, but he loves the thrill of reeling it in.

Other times, a cat isn't playing at all. She's just inexperienced. Although kittens are born hunters, they aren't necessarily good at it. To get good, they need practice. That's why mother cats bring home live prey for their kittens to kill. Pet kittens that miss this training often grow up rather poor at the job.

The other problem cats face is fear. Prey animals make dangerous opponents. They have claws, beaks, or teeth. To avoid being injured, a cat tires out whatever animal she catches. Then it can't fight back when she goes in for the kill. So what looks like torture to us makes good cat sense.

Cats are such **good mousers** that, during the California gold rush, miners paid £40 apiece for them. That's £800 in today's money.

DISAPPEARING ACT

It breaks your heart. Your cat eats breakfast, goes outside, and never returns. You cry, picturing him stolen, lost in the woods, or trapped in the jaws of a vicious dog. Such tragedies do happen. But much of the time, kitties leave on purpose.

This sounds strange because cats are natural homebodies. They bond to their territory as well as their people. Some home-loving cats go so far as to return to their old neighbourhoods after their families have moved away.

So why would others abandon their turf? A sick, elderly feline might instinctively slip away to hide, like her ancestors did to avoid predators. If she dies in hiding, her grieving owners may never know what happened.

Healthy cats that haven't been spayed or neutered are famous for wandering off. They are searching for mates and eventually return on their own. But other cats have to be tracked down. These pets run away because they're unhappy at home. Either they don't like the food, or they're fighting with other cats.

If your cat keeps leaving, get him neutered, protect him from other animals, or start keeping him inside. Some cat lovers build their pets a big outdoor pen out of wood and chicken wire, with shelves and branches to climb on. You must change something, or a wandering cat won't stay.

When **Porsche** the cat went missing during Superstorm Sandy, his family feared he was gone forever. But six months later, he turned up **back home.**

DR. GARY'S VET TIPS

ALL CATS should be microchipped and wear an ID tag on a break-away collar if they go outside. If your cat does disappear, tack up posters around the neighbourhood and bring some to all the local animal shelters. Include contact information, a photo of your cat, and a reward. Some folks have had good luck by posting "missing cat" notices on Facebook and other social media. Also prop open a door; maybe he'll return on his own. Remember to ask around at shelters, too! Less than 10 percent of people who are missing a cat check their local shelter. We end up with a lot of strays that no one is looking for.

ANTISOCIAL KITTY

Friendly cats like most people. Scaredy-cats don't like any people. And fussy cats only like certain people. Whether cats are shy or bold depends on two things: the genes they inherit from their parents and how much they were handled, or socialized, as kittens. Of the two, handling is more important. And it must take place before the kittens turn eight weeks old. Otherwise, they'll grow up wild.

So if your cat only goes to your mother, don't feel bad. There isn't anything wrong with you. It's because only one person spent time with your cat when she was little.

If you want a cuddly cat that's attached to you, adopt a kitten. A kitten will get to know you by watching your body language. Then she will tailor her personality to fit yours. Once cats are a year old, their personalities are set and unlikely to change.

Suppose you already have a nervous adult cat. She follows you around and sits beside you on the couch, but always keeps her distance. She doesn't like being stroked and won't sit on your lap. Leave her be! Don't bug her by chasing her around and always trying to pick her up. In fact, ignore her. Give her some space, and let her choose when to come to you. One day, when you least expect it, she will.

Caregivers at the kitten nursery run by the San Diego Humane Society and SPCA socialize up to 2,000 homeless cat babies a year so they'll make good pets.

THIS IS NICE, BUT DON'T COME ANY CLOSER.

DR. GARY'S VET TIPS

SHOULD YOU keep your cat inside or let him go out? It's a tough question all cat owners face. The simple answer is that cats are safer living indoors. That's because outdoor cats risk death or injury from outdoor dangers, can get infected from parasites and fleas, and can get lost or stolen. But indoor cats aren't immune to risk. They still need to be vaccinated against diseases. And a lack of exercise often causes weight gain, which can lead to diabetes. Equally serious is the fact that some cats simply can't stand being cooped up. Left unable to hunt and explore makes them bored and anxious, and the stress can cause urinary troubles and behavioural issues. So listen to your cat. If he's happy and healthy kept inside, great. But if indoor living is driving him crazy, compromise. Let him out during the day, but bring him in at night. Every cat is an individual. Make the decision that's best for the one you love.

C'MON. IS THIS THE BEST YOU'VE GOT?

DR. GARY'S VET TIPS

BE EXTREMELY careful if you ever think of cooking your own cat food. It's very difficult. And never try to turn your cat into a vegetarian. Cats' dietary needs are so specific that missing just one nutrient can sicken or even kill them. Most important, cats must have meat. As for kitty treats, they're all pretty much the same. Just don't give your cat too many or she may join the 58 percent of pet cats that are overweight. Then she'll run the risk of developing arthritis and diabetes.

PICKY EATER

Many cats have expensive tastes. They turn up their nose at dry food and insist on canned. Or they want a different flavor at every meal. The cat that demands variety may simply be spoiled. But one that only eats canned food is wise. Canned food usually contains more meat and more water. The water is important for cats, who tend to drink very little, and meat contains protein. Protein is an important nutrient, especially for cats. They need five times as much as dogs do, which is why cats can't survive on dog food. A lack of protein makes cats go blind and causes heart disease.

In the wild, cats get their meat from eating mice—the *purr*-fect food.

But pet cats that are kept inside and not allowed to hunt are at risk. So it's up to us to feed them right. But suppose you do, and your fussy feline refuses to eat. Here are some things to try:

If other cats live in the house, make sure the non-eater is not being bullied. Try changing his food, moving his dish to a quieter spot, or feeding him from a saucer instead of a bowl. If you've been giving your cat refrigerated food, let it warm up first. It will smell stronger. But don't wait more than two days before seeing the vet. Your kitty might have sore gums or infected teeth, and sick cats can go downhill fast.

A Persian cat once ate its owner's diamond-and-ruby ring worth £3,700!

WHAT IS THIS CaT SAYING?

The Scenario

Eleven-year-old Hannah already had one cat, Angel, when her father gave her another. The new cat was a mischievous gray tabby named Rascal. As often happens, the two unrelated cats took an instant dislike to each other.

Neva masquerade

British shorthair

Angel panicked and tried to ward off the intruder by marking her territory. She peed on Hannah's parents' bed, leaving big yellow stains on their expensive down comforter. Did this scare Rascal away? No. If anything, it made him more aggressive.

Rascal began hiding behind the couch and ambushing Angel whenever she walked by. "One time, Rascal had Angel's neck in his mouth," Hannah says. "He was on top of Angel kicking and clawing her with his hind feet." Hannah broke up that fight by stomping on the floor.

But the damage was done. Rascal became the top cat. He soon took over the living room and frightened Angel into spending most of her time hiding upstairs. She only came out to eat and use her litter box. Hannah felt bad. She knew Angel was miserable. But she loved both her kitties and could not imagine giving either one away. Clearly, somebody had to do something.

You Be the Expert

What's going on here? Why doesn't Angel defend herself, and why is Rascal acting like such a bully?

Cats can get badly injured in a fight. Angel has already lost one battle, and she knows better than to push her luck. Hiding makes her feel safe.

As for Rascal, he could feel as confident as he acts. But it's more likely that he doesn't. A feline bully either wants to get something, like food, treats, or territory, from his victim, or he himself is anxious and stressed. Remember, Rascal was suddenly thrust into another, older cat's territory. Maybe he feared he had to take a stand or Angel would bully him!

Getting Cats to Call a Truce

Hannah's grandparents bought her a cat tree, two fishing pole–type cat toys, and a bag of treats. Then Hannah went to work. She rubbed a cloth on Angel's back to pick up her scent and rubbed the cloth on the tree. Every night, she played with both cats, at the same time. She gave them each a treat afterward. Rascal played rough and broke his toy the first week. This forced both cats to bat at the same feathered mouse. To Hannah's surprise, neither seemed to mind. The two rivals were willing to play together to get their treats.

Then, one night, Hannah went downstairs and saw both cats sharing the tree! Angel was on the middle branch and Rascal was on the top.

SCRITCH, SCRATCH

Teaching your cat to use a scratching post

 Cats scratch. Scratching keeps their nails in shape, and it feels good. So if you want to protect the furniture, don't wait. Install a scratching post as soon as you bring your kitty home.

 Buy or make a new one. Cats don't like to share and won't use a secondhand post that has been used by other felines.

 Locate the post in your kitty's favourite room in the house.

 Offer both a flat and an upright surface. Cats love having a choice.

 The upright surface must be at least three feet (91 cm) high, so your kitty can stretch up tall when using it.

 To attract your cat to the post, try sprinkling catnip on top and around the base. Some cats love that. But if yours doesn't, use food treats or staple strings or a cat toy to the top—whatever turns her on.

FeLINE FEELINGS

WHAT IS IT ABOUT CATS? They don't help with search and rescue or do what we say. They wander off without us and ignore us when we call. Yet we adore cats for their soft fur, baby faces, and independent nature. The fact that befriending one is like taming a tiger only makes us love them more.

As different as cats are from us, they share our feelings. Scientists used to think that wasn't so. But high-tech brain imaging machines prove that cats have the same mental makeup for producing emotions that humans have. What's more, they home in on and respond to how we're feeling. There are countless true stories of individual cats helping humans through trying times. Tilly, a timid rescue cat, suddenly came out of her shell and comforted her owner when both she and her husband were diagnosed with cancer. And the love of an Afghanistan stray helped a soldier recover from the devastating deaths of two of his friends.

Our cats are there for us, and we can be there for them—if we know how they feel.

CHECK OUT THE
FELINES!

WANT TO SEE cats in action?
Check out these blue boxes on each
page for Web addresses for some of
the best videos of cat emotion.

Colourpoint shorthair

ALERT

One benefit of owning a cat is that you always have a sentry on duty. People tend to think of dogs as guarding the house. But cats also do an excellent job. They have better hearing than dogs and remain on standby—even when they appear to be snoozing.

Let anything out of the ordinary occur—a rustling noise, a gust of wind, or an unusual odour—and *zing!* A cat instantly shifts into high alert. Her eyes pop open, her muscles tense, and her ears stand up. She may flick her tail as she watches, listens, and sniffs—ready for action. That's a good thing. Just ask Jon and Deyn Johnson, of Estes Park, Colorado, U.S.A. On the night of September 14, 2013, they were in bed asleep. They didn't know that the Big Thompson River had flooded its banks. They didn't hear the torrent of water rushing toward them. But

Jezebel did. She jumped on Jon. Then she yowled and batted his face until he woke up. It was just in time. Deyn leaped out of bed and water rose halfway to her knees. The couple grabbed Jezebel and ran to warn the vacationers staying in their rental cottages. The cottages washed away, like most of the town. But the Johnsons and their guests survived, thanks to Jezebel, their light-sleeping watch cat.

CHECK OUT THE FELINES!

THIS TV-WATCHING cat can't hear the dramatic background music that someone has added for effect, but he certainly hears something startling!

FROM YOUTUBE:
tinyurl.com/howtospeakcatalert

Some **scientists** believe cats can hear the ultrasonic sounds that come before an **earthquake.**

HAPPY

They're everywhere. Happy cats live in houses and university halls of residences, on farms and in city flats. They even roll along in caravans and motorhomes and serve as shipmates on boats.

You can tell a happy cat by his loose, relaxed body; half-perked ears; and droopy whiskers. He'll greet you with a chipper "Hi, there" miaow and a straight-up tail. Then he'll jump on your lap, purr loudly, and move his body under your hand so that you stroke him where he likes it best.

Cats need very little—just food, shelter, and protection from their enemies. They don't require company and usually prefer being "only" cats.

What cats do want is plenty to do and freedom of choice. One couple gave their cats both by turning their whole house in San Diego, California, into a kitty playground. It features a hot pink spiral staircase that leads to a boardwalk built high on the walls, a floor-to-ceiling scratching post, look-out spots, tunnels, ramps, and hidey-holes. Both cats and human visitors love it.

But you don't need anything that elaborate. You can give an outdoor kitty more choice by installing a cat door into your garden. For an indoor cat, simply put a pillow on a top shelf and arrange the furniture so that he can reach it. Your beloved pet will adore you for it.

DR. GARY'S VET TIPS

NAMES MATTER. To choose a good one for your cat, play with him for a few days first. Then you can pick a name that matches his personality, like "Trouble" for a mischievous male cat or "Missy" for a dainty female. You can also go for something that describes his looks. One solid white cat with a stubby tail is called "Whitey-bob". Whatever you choose, keep it short. Scientists have discovered that cats respond best to two-syllable names that end with the "y" or "ie" sound. "Charlie", "Lucy", "Smokey", and "Daisy" are some currently popular cat names that work especially well.

Sir Isaac Newton,
the British scientist who discovered gravity in 1687, also invented the cat door.

AHH... THIS IS THE LIFE.

CHECK OUT THE FELINES!

WATCH THESE happy cats in their whole-home playground in this video of "The Cats' House", created by Bob Walker.

FROM DISCOVERY'S ANIMAL PLANET:
tinyurl.com/howtospeakcathappy

PLAYFUL

Kittens are always in the mood for fun. They spend almost every waking minute playing. At about seven weeks old, kittens learn the signs for inviting each other to take part. They can make a play-face, roll onto their backs, or stand up on their hind legs. Holding their tail like a question mark, arching their back, and hopping sideways might be other ways. Curling their tail upward, arching their back, and leaping straight up, however, mean they're "all done".

Adult cats don't play with other cats. They only play with toys. And they don't play long. Many cats romp for two minutes tops, before walking away—and for good reason. It turns out that what looks like playing to us is really hunting in the mind of a cat.

Here's proof: A cat plays longer and harder if he's hungry, if his toy is mouse-size, and if it's made of fur or feathers. Most important is that the toy must fall apart! If a cat attacks and thinks all his biting and clawing will win him a meal, he keeps at it. But, if the toy appears indestructible and nothing changes, the poor kitty gives up in frustration. Think about that. It's just as important to give your cat a treat at the end of each game, as it is to play with him in the first place.

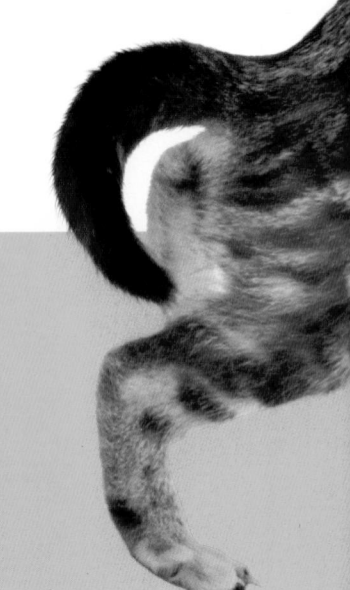

CHECK OUT THE FELINES!

A KITTEN plays energetically, clawing, pawing, and sideways hopping—with a young pitbull—in this endearing video from a site with lots of fun pet videos!

FROM PAW BONITO:
tinyurl.com/howtospeakcatplayful

Cats multiply fast. Dusty, a Texas, U.S.A., tabby, holds the record for birthing the most kittens—420 in 18 years!

BORED

Until the 1980s, most everyone let their cats outside. Contented kitties basked in the sun. They explored their territories, leaving scent messages. And they hunted. Outdoor cats led adventurous lives. They were rarely, if ever, bored.

But life can get dull for indoor cats. They're like tigers in the zoo. While captive cats may have soft beds and tasty food, they're still stuck in a cage. They can't choose whether to go in or out, hunt or play. Experts say that up to 40 percent of today's pet felines fall into a "blue funk" and do nothing but eat and sleep. Others misbehave and cause trouble.

If your cat is fat, sleeps more than 18 hours a day, or misbehaves, give her more to do. Indoor cats need scratching posts, hiding spots, window seats, puzzle toys, and maybe even clicker training. They also need to play-hunt. Just leaving a catnip mouse on the floor won't do it. Toys must move to trigger a cat's hunting instinct, so you must get involved. Otherwise, your bored kitty might liven things up by pouncing on you and biting your ankles!

The average cat lives about **15 years,** but some have survived into their 30s.

CHECK OUT THE FELINES!

THE HEAL VETERINARY HOSPITAL, in Dallas, Texas, U.S.A., posted this inspiring video to show how the staff helped a fat cat named Skinny lose 17 pounds (8 kg). He went from being barely able to walk to actually running.

FROM YOUTUBE:
tinyurl.com/howtospeakcatbored

BOOORING. THERE'S NOTHING TO DO AROUND HERE.

Persian

DR. GARY'S VET TIPS

MOST CATS don't like other cats. So forcing unrelated cats to live together can be a very bad idea. But siblings usually remain friends for life. So if you don't have a cat and are thinking about adopting one, consider getting two littermates. They'll keep each other company. If you already have a cat that needs a friend, start by fostering another cat from an animal shelter. If the two hit it off, great! If they don't, you can return the foster. This way you're letting your first cat in on the decision.

DEPRESSED or GRIEF-STRICKEN

Buffy the keeshond puppy and Jitters the cat lived together for seven years. One night, Buffy got hurt, laid down on the carpet, and died. Next time Jitters entered that room she sniffed that spot and laid down on it. Every evening, for weeks afterward, she slept in that exact same spot.

Another cat, named Stripe, had trouble adjusting when his teenage owner left for college. He looked for his owner for days and took to sitting outside the boy's closed bedroom door, miaowing pitifully. When the boy didn't return, Stripe moved to a corner of the bathroom, where he just stared at the wall.

Were these cats suffering from grief and depression? Experts disagree, but cats bond deeply to people and other animals, so it makes sense that they would feel their loss. Even if that loss is due to being pushed aside by a rival cat. A sad cat crouches low, wraps her tail around herself, and lowers her ears. Her whiskers droop. Some stop grooming or quit using the litter box. In 1996, a study found that 65 percent of cats significantly changed their behaviour after a companion's death. They ate less, miaowed more, slept more, and acted "clingy" with their owners.

Grief can last six months. But if your cat stops eating or becomes withdrawn, thin, and messy looking, she could be depressed. Take her to the vet. Some cats need the same medications that help people, or the vet might recommend an animal behaviourist who can help. Just don't give up. With proper care, depressed humans recover and so do kitties.

Some cats reach out to sad people, rubbing up against their legs to make them feel better.

Persian

CHECK OUT THE
FELINES!

IN THIS video posted by a pet owner, a grieving cat fondles the collar of his doggie friend that recently passed away.

FROM YOUTUBE:
tinyurl.com/howtospeakcatgrief

PLEASE HELP. I CAN'T TAKE THIS ANYMORE.

DR. GARY'S VET TIPS

CATS DON'T like each other, and some will never be happy unless they can be the "only" cat. It's heartbreaking but true. When cats aren't getting along, we usually recommend that people give them each a safe place to hide and then wait a few months. Sometimes the cats can work it out. But if they can't, you'll have to make the hard decision. It's best if you can find another home, with one of your friends or family, for one of your cats yourself. If all else fails, it might be better to take him to a shelter than have him live in fear at home.

ANXIOUS

Emotions direct animal behaviour. Any cat that sees a rival cat coming immediately gets anxious. That anxiety, or worry, over something that hasn't happened yet, propels her into action. She may have wide eyes, lick and swallow, turn her ears back, and wrap her tail tightly around herself. She'll crouch down and lie flat, tensing her body and preparing to flee. An anxious cat won't make a sound. This gut-level response is temporary and helps an animal survive.

Chronic, or long-lasting, anxiety does the opposite. It can weaken a cat's health and ruin her ability to live a full life. The same things that upset humans—like divorce, moving, remarriage, or a death in the family—stress out cats. So can dirty litter boxes, a new carpet, guests in the house, or a lack of hiding places. But the most common cause is another cat—either a neighbour cat or a rival in her own house. Cats can live together without fighting and still mistrust each other.

A stressed cat might start spraying or pooing outside her litter box in a desperate attempt to spread her scent around and reclaim her territory. You can help by playing with her more. That will distract her and build her confidence. Some experts recommend a plug-in scent diffuser, like "Feliway". Feliway is aroma therapy for cats. It produces a calming odour that smells like a cat's facial glands. It may not work in all cases, but it may be worth a try.

CHECK OUT THE FELINES!

AN ANXIOUS kitty worries about what will happen at the pet salon in this video from a professional cat groomer.

FROM YOUTUBE:
tinyurl.com/howtospeakcatanxious

Prozac and other anti-anxiety drugs developed for humans also help cats.

CHECK OUT THE
FELINES!

A FRUSTRATED cat tries in vain to catch a bird outside the window in this video posted by a pet owner.

FROM YOUTUBE:
tinyurl.com/howtospeakcatfrustrated

IT'S NOT FAIR! I'M STUCK IN HERE!

Persian

FRUSTRATED

Hard, wide eyes; forward, pricked ears; batting paws; chattering teeth; and a slowly thrashing tail. That's a frustrated cat. Like humans, cats get frustrated when they don't get what they expect. It happens a lot. An indoor cat stares out the window at a bird or passing feline. But he can't reach it. The longer he sits and watches, the greater his frustration, until he's ready to attack someone—maybe you.

A shelter cat is put into a cage and surrounded by strange smells, noises, people, and animals. Relaxed kitties can cope. Frustrated ones can't. They watch, pace, bite their handlers, and get physically sick. That's right. Constant frustration lowers a cat's immune system, making him more prone to infections.

A playful cat tries to catch the moving light from a laser pen. It can be amusing to watch. But imagine how it feels to stalk and pounce—to the point of exhaustion—and never catch the thing! The terrible frustration gives some cats an incurable compulsive disorder.

So what can we do? We can tape cardboard over a window to block a cat's view. Shelter workers can identify frustrated cats so vets and shelter staff can take preventive measures to protect their health. And we can use fishing-pole toys instead of laser pens and always let our cat catch the "mouse" at the end (or throw him a treat when he catches the laser!).

Some Siamese and other Oriental cat breeds develop a compulsion to suck and eat wool.

SCARED

Some are more timid than others. But let's face it. Cats can be wimps. Anything from loud noises to strangers at the door might make them bolt. Given a choice, cats always prefer to escape. But when they can't, they mask their fear. Maybe, on Monday, you pull out the nail clippers. Your kitty crouches on the floor, tucks in his tail, ducks his head, flattens his ears, and pulls back his whiskers. Why? He's trying to look smaller, even invisible.

Then, on Tuesday, your cat sees the neighbour's dog. This time he tries to look bigger! He stiffens his legs, stands on tiptoe, and puffs out his hair. Then he arches his back and either sticks his bristly tail straight up or hangs it down like a question mark. He also growls, hisses, and spits. It's the same emotion expressed two different ways. No wonder owners get confused.

Sometimes you can cure a scaredy-cat by desensitizing him. Desensitizing works like allergy shots. It gets a cat used to something in tiny doses. Suppose your cat is afraid of the vacuum. Play with him while somebody else vacuums a far-off room. Each day, move the vacuum a little closer, until cat and cleaner are in the same room. Now, keep the cleaner off. Don't turn it back on until your kitty's fine with it. This is a slow process requiring tons of patience. But it can be done.

DR. GARY'S VET TIPS

DON'T TRY to pick up and comfort a frightened cat. She's likely to claw you or even bite. Just talk to her in a calm, reassuring voice and remove whatever it is that's scaring her. As soon as she thinks it's safe enough, she'll run and hide. Or she may slowly slink away, one paw at a time, with her body hugging the ground. Leave her be. After she has calmed down—which may take hours— she'll reappear. You can stroke her then.

The word for cat is
mao in Chinese,
gatto in Italian, *poes* in Dutch,
and *kedi* in Turkish.

YIKES! I'VE GOT TO GET OUT OF HERE.

CHECK OUT THE FELINES!

THIS PET owner's black cat shows some classic scaredy-cat behaviour while spooky music plays in the background.

FROM YOUTUBE:
tinyurl.com/howtospeakcatscared

ANGRY or AGGRESSIVE

Most of the time, cats act calm and laid back. They only act out when they're very afraid or really angry. Then they arch their backs, fluff up their tails, and hiss. Fear and anger look the same at first, because all cats fear fighting and will do everything they can to bluff their way out of it. So stay away and don't touch them!

If the bluff fails, a cat will raise his ears and growl a threat. Things escalate from there. Besides trying to look big, an angry cat swivels his ears around, points his whiskers forward, and lowers his head. He stares directly at his opponent—usually another cat—with fixed, narrow pupils. At first, the angry cat's tail might twitch at the tip. But the madder he gets, the faster it moves. Then his ears flatten, his growls turn to caterwauling, and he creeps forward, almost in slow motion.

Some disputes end in staring contests. Others deteriorate into paw-slapping matches. The worst result is a brawl. Like boxers in a ring, two cats will circle each other, repeatedly approaching and backing off, before one launches a full-scale attack.

Cat fights are serious. Most happen after midnight, so you may have heard but probably haven't seen one. They usually end with two unhappy cats—both bloodied and needing the care of a vet.

CHECK OUT THE FELINES!

THIS PET owner made a video of two enemy cats paw-slapping each other. It may look like the hand game patty-cake, but it's actually a fight!

FROM YOUTUBE:
tinyurl.com/howtospeakcatangry

Many cats hold grudges, but some feline housemates manage to "lick and make up".

Burmese

HOW DARE YOU TRY TO STEAL MY TURF!

DR. GARY'S VET TIPS

CAT SCRATCHES and bites can go unnoticed, because they're difficult to find. Often a cat will just be limping, and you can't see any wound. But it's there. So, always carefully check your cat for injuries if he's been in a fight. Cat bites often form an abscess, which is like a big, infected pimple full of pus. Abscesses are very painful and must be drained and treated with antibiotics to prevent serious infection. To prevent fights, keep your cat inside at night.

HE CAN'T HEAR ME COMING.

DR. GARY'S VET TIPS

EVEN FERAL cats rarely survive by hunting alone. All around the world, millions of people help feed them. In America, some animal shelters sponsor community cat programs through which homeless cats are returned to the wild and fed by volunteers. One man became so attached to a cat colony that moved into his vacant garage that he left money to care for them after he died. Those cats now live at California's Folsom City Sanctuary Zoo, where the feral cat exhibit is the first one visitors see when they enter zoo grounds. It's also amazingly popular.

ON the HUNT

Shhh! This cat is after something. You can tell by his intense stare, forward-pointing ears and whiskers, and twitching tail. All his senses are alert as he pads silently toward his prey, crouching low to the ground.

Cats closely guard their home territory, but they don't mind sharing their hunting range. A hunting range is a series of trails that lead to good lookout spots. Cats take turns visiting them at different times. Still, every cat hunts alone, just like his African wildcat ancestors did.

Hunting is difficult, dangerous work. Humans used to admire cats for their courage and skill at it. Without cats, early Egyptians would have lost much of their food supply to rats. Sailors took the little rodent killers to sea with them, spreading the animals around the world. As recently as 100 years ago, farmers everywhere welcomed cats with open arms.

But today, we control rats with pesticides and traps. Let a cat drop a partly eaten mouse at our feet, and we turn away in disgust. We now expect cats to just give up hunting and become cuddly house pets instead. Some scientists think this is asking too much. They say we should let our cats be cats or else figure out how to breed cats that don't need to hunt. It isn't fair to just expect felines to suddenly change their ways.

CHECK OUT THE FELINES!

THIS CLIP shows a scene from a nature documentary featuring a feral cat that hunts pigeons.

FROM YOUTUBE, BBC VIDEO:
tinyurl.com/howtospeakcathunt

Cats hunt what they can get: rabbits in the UK, lizards in Georgia, U.S.A., and baby turtles on Africa's Seychelles Islands.

WHAT IS THIS CaT SAYING?

The Scenario

Tommy Tittlemouse, a pudgy black-and-white cat, lived in a house in Utica, New York. Phoebe, the lady who lived next door, liked Tommy and Tommy liked her. She scratched him behind the ears and fed him occasional table scraps. Tommy spent so much time sitting on Phoebe's front steps that he attracted the attention of a passerby, who stopped to chat.

"Your cat is pregnant," the woman announced.

"No, *he* isn't," Phoebe said. "He's just fat, and besides, he's not mine."

The know-it-all stranger stomped off in a huff. "I know a pregnant cat when I see one," she said.

No, she didn't. But she was right about one thing. Tommy would soon belong to Phoebe, part-time anyway. Rather than service a litter box, Tommy's owners always put him outside at bedtime. One stormy night, Phoebe awoke to the sound of Tommy miaowing. She got up, went over to her bedroom window and looked out. Tommy was huddled on a nearby tree branch, soaking wet and shivering. Phoebe didn't hesitate. She opened the window and Tommy jumped in.

That did it. From then on, Tommy lived in two places. He spent his days with his official owners and his nights curled up on the foot of Phoebe's bed. Phoebe, of course, knew all about his two-timing. But his other owners? They never had a clue.

You Be the Expert

Why did Tommy start staying at Phoebe's? What did he want, or need, that he wasn't getting at home?

Cats look out for themselves. Some get run out of their homes by a rival cat. Others hate the food, don't feel safe, or are stuck with a feline roommate that they don't like. So they seek out better arrangements. In this case, Tommy wanted more attention and a warm, comfortable place to sleep.

Two-timing kitties are more common than you think. In 2011, National Geographic and the University of Georgia conducted a research project on cats. Fifty-five outdoor kitties wore little cameras attached to their collars. When the researchers reviewed the photos, they were surprised. Four of those 55 cats lived with two families, getting food and affection from each!

How to Know If a Cat Is Stray?

Suppose a strange cat starts hanging around your house. Before adopting him, you want to be sure he doesn't belong to somebody else. Here are two ways to find out.

1. Take a digital picture of him and print it out on some leaflets asking if anyone owns him. Distribute the leafletets around your neighbourhood.
2. Cut a strip of paper to length. Write on it, "If found, please call," and print your phone number. Tie it around the cat's neck.

INSIDE, OUTSIDE, OR OPEN, SESAME!

Teach your cat to use a cat door.

 1 Give your cat time to get used to the door. If you push her through, you might frighten her for life. Start by clipping a clothes peg to the door up near the hinge. This will prop it open so your kitty can see through it.

 2 Have someone hold your cat outside the door while you stay inside. Call her by name and show her a treat. Give her the treat the minute she comes through.

 3 Once your cat is coming in by herself, reverse the process. Leave her inside and call her to come out. Treat her when she does.

 4 Gradually lower the door by moving the clothes peg down. When you remove the clothes peg altogether, smear butter on the bottom door edge. That will entice your kitty to push it open with her head. Call her from the other side. This could take weeks, but it's worth it—for you and your cat.

Ragdoll

MEET AND
GREET

INTRODUCING A NEW CaT TO THE CaT YOU ALREADY HAVE

1 If possible, bring your new kitty home in a cat carrier, not holding her loose in your arms. Take her straight into a bathroom, or some other "safe room". Put a cardboard box lined with a towel in there, along with a bowl of water, cat toys, and a litter box. Set the carrier on the floor, open it, put a kitty treat nearby, and leave. Keep the safe room door closed.

2 Next day, find a pair of socks. Slip your hand into one and rub it gently all over your first cat's face. Leave that sock in the safe room. Then rub the other sock on your new kitty, and leave that with your first cat. Do this for three or four days, using clean socks each time.

3 Once your cats are familiar with each other's scents, have them switch rooms. By sniffing and exploring, they'll learn even more.

4 Bring your kitties face-to-face, except keep the new one safely shut inside her carrier. Don't worry if they hiss. Now feed them both. Be sure to give your first cat something really yummy, and let her see the caged kitty while she eats. Both cats will begin to think that good things happen when they are together. Repeat several times.

5 Finally, let the new kitty out of her carrier to eat. Feed your other cat at the same time, but in a far corner of the room. Keep the carrier and safe room doors open, so the new kitty can escape if necessary. With luck, your kitties will eventually become friends.

CaT MYTHS BUSTED

SUPERSTITION: Black cats bring bad luck.

HOW IT MAY HAVE BEGUN: During the Middle Ages—between the 5th and 15th centuries—many Europeans blamed witches when things went wrong. People accused of being witches were usually female, and many of them kept pet cats. That started a rumor that black cats could be witches in disguise.

WHY IT ISN'T TRUE: First of all, there's no such thing as a witch—human or animal. Second, the colour of a cat can't make it evil. Just ask Maria Gillon, 14, of Scotland. Maria suffers from potentially deadly heart seizures, especially when she's sleeping at night. Her solid black cat, Perla, sleeps with her and alerts Maria's mother whenever her daughter's heart stops beating. Perla has saved Maria's life several times, and Maria knows she is lucky to have her.

SUPERSTITION: Milk is good for cats.

HOW IT MAY HAVE BEGUN: For years, many dairy farmers kept colonies of barn cats. The cats killed mice and rats, and the farmers thanked them by setting out pans of milk.

WHY IT ISN'T TRUE: Mother's milk is great for kittens. But after they're weaned, many cats (like some people) lose the ability to digest lactose—the sugar found in milk. Barn cats are wild, so the farmers didn't notice. But drinking milk makes many cats vomit or have diarrhea. They are much healthier when they eat mice or are fed commercial cat food.

SUPERSTITION: Curiosity killed the cat.

HOW IT MAY HAVE BEGUN: Cats are famous for exploring. They spend lots of time poking around and sticking their heads (and sometimes their whole bodies) into openings. Anything that moves, makes a strange noise, or smells different attracts their attention.

WHY IT ISN'T TRUE: As nosy as cats are, they're also cautious. Watch and you will see a cat reach out and carefully touch

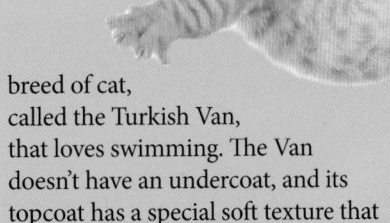

something with one paw to test what happens. Still, cats sometimes make mistakes and venture where they shouldn't. One curious feline got stuck inside a vending machine for 37 days! Another spent three days trapped inside a drainpipe. Yet a third crawled inside his owner's suitcase and ended up flying from Ohio, U.S.A., to Florida. All of these cats survived, proving that their curiosity didn't kill them. It did make their lives more interesting, however!

SUPERSTITION: All cats hate water.

HOW IT MAY HAVE BEGUN: Most people come to this conclusion from personal observation. Cats hate baths. They also don't jump in the pool with us and doggy paddle around.

WHY IT ISN'T TRUE: All cats can swim, tigers included. Most house cats simply prefer not to, because the water soaks through both their topcoat and their undercoat, and it takes them hours to lick themselves dry. But there is one breed of cat, called the Turkish Van, that loves swimming. The Van doesn't have an undercoat, and its topcoat has a special soft texture that makes it water resistant.

SUPERSTITION: Cats always land on their feet.

HOW IT MAY HAVE BEGUN: Sugar, a white cat in Boston, Massachusetts, U.S.A., survived a 19-story fall, with no serious injuries! Miracle stories like this led to another myth that cats have nine lives, which also isn't true.

WHY IT ISN'T TRUE: A very flexible spine and no collarbone allow cats to right themselves in midair, with nothing to push against. A falling cat can also spread its legs and slow its fall by "parachuting" down. As remarkable as both these tricks are, they take time to do. Studies show that cats that fall from greater heights (seven stories and up) actually fare better than those that tumble off a second-floor balcony. Either way, a fall is not a good thing, and many cats don't survive, superstition or not!

WE ♥ THEM; WE ♥ THEM NOT

A HISTORY OF HUMANS' ON AGAIN/ OFF AGAIN LOVE AFFAIR WITH CaTS

> Early humans, on the isle of Cyprus (south of Turkey), bury a person and a cat in the same grave. This is the earliest fossil evidence of human beings loving and living with feline companions.

> Ancient Persia takes advantage of the fact that Egyptians worship the goddess Bastet, who is thought to take the form of a cat. When the Persian army attacks an Egyptian city, every soldier carries a live cat as a shield. Unwilling to harm the sacred animals, the Egyptians surrender.

ABOUT 7500 B.C.	1450 B.C.	500 B.C.

> Ancient Egyptians love and tame cats. They even mummify them when they die. But they haven't named them, until now. The first cat ever known to have a name is called "Nadjem", which means "pleasant one". We know because his name is inscribed on his owner's tomb.

> Cats are pampered and kept on leashes in Japan, where only royalty can own them. But when hordes of rats start eating the grain and silkworms, the emperor passes a decree. All cats must be freed. And it works! The cats save the crops and the silk.

> In Egypt, a Muslim sultan (the ruler of Egypt and Syria) founds the first cat sanctuary. He wills the income from his orchard to the homeless cats of Cairo, and for centuries afterward street cats receive a free meal every day.

A.D. 1200	1280	1484	1620

> The Pilgrims bring cats with them on the *Mayflower*, when they sail to the New World. They also bring pigs, goats, chickens, sheep, rabbits, caged birds, and two dogs.

> Pope Innocent VIII proclaims that cats are witches in disguise. As a result, all over Europe, cats are tortured and killed on sight. Their persecution continues for two hundred years.

159

> The Cat in the Hat—
a funny story
starring a top-
hatted, bow-tied
cat—is published.
Author Theodor
Geisel, also known as
Dr. Seuss, wrote the
book to help children
learn to read. Today
it's one of the top ten
all-time best-selling
children's books.

> Psychologist Zing Yang Kuo
discovers that kittens raised
with rats never kill any rats
that they have grown up with.
Nor will cats kill rabbits, mice,
or birds if they lived with them
when they were kittens under
the age of two months old.

> Bob, the beloved kitty of famous
author Charles Dickens, dies.
Dickens is devastated. Taxidermy
is popular, so Dickens has one of
Bob's front paws stuffed and
attached to the blade of an ivory
letter opener. He keeps the
paw-handled opener on his desk
in memory of his friend.

| **1862** | **1871** | **1930** | **1957** | **1963** |

> The world's first cat show takes
place in London, England.
A group of "cat fanciers"
(people who keep cats as pets,
not mousers) arrange for 170
cats to be on exhibit. Eighteen
years later, three times as many
cats are shown before a crowd
of 20,000 fanciers.

> Felicette, a black-and-
white French feline,
becomes the first cat in
space. She rockets more
than 100 miles (161 km)
above Earth and returns
home the same day.
Her fast flight helps
scientists learn more
about weightlessness and
the rigors of space travel.

> In the United States, pet cats outnumber pet dogs for the first time. There are 81.7 million cats, compared with 72.1 million dogs. With more people moving from the country into the city each year, experts expect this trend to continue.

> Tommaso, a four-year-old stray cat adopted by a wealthy Italian woman, becomes the richest cat in the world. Italian law forbade his 94-year-old, childless owner from leaving her multimillion pound estate to him directly. So the elderly lady willed her money and her cat to a woman she trusted to take good care of him.

1978   2007   2011   2014

> Garfield, a lazy orange cat, first appears in a newspaper cartoon strip. He's named after creator Jim Davis's grandfather and is based on an assortment of barn cats that Davis grew up with on an Indiana, U.S.A., farm. Today, Garfield is seen in 131 countries (including China) and read by 200 million people.

> Body Armour for cats goes on sale. Hand-stitched from black leather, this gladiator-style get-up is supposed to protect your kitty from dogs, coyotes, and rival cats. It costs £400 and might work— if you can manage to get your cat into it.

SOFT & FURRY CaTs

(EVEN CATS THAT HAVE NO HAIR!)

Cats make excellent mousers. They are so good that there's little room for improvement. So humans left them alone to do their thing. Then, in the mid-1800s, world travellers began bringing unusual-looking cats back to England. And the English noticed. They began separating cats into breeds as with dogs. Only cat breeds weren't designed to do specific jobs. Breeds were based solely on beauty. Today, we have about 50. Check out some of our most striking and best-loved ones!

AMERICAN SHORTHAIR

HOMELAND Descended from cats brought to America by European settlers during colonial times

IDENTIFYING FEATURES Tough and hardy, with a muscular body, round eyes in a round head, and a short, dense coat. Skilled mousers, they come in more than 80 colours and coat patterns.

FUN TO KNOW The American shorthair is the pedigreed version of the everyday cat that most of us know and love. The Pilgrims brought the ancestors of these ship cats with them to America on the *Mayflower*. Some of the furry immigrants might even have arrived earlier, in 1607, with the Jamestown settlers.

MAINE COON

HOMELAND North America

IDENTIFYING FEATURES Big, up to 18 pounds (8 kg), with a long, plumed tail; thick, shaggy coat; and a distinctive ruff of fur around the neck

FUN TO KNOW Cosey, a brown tabby Maine coon won the first North American cat show, held in New York City's Madison Square Garden on May 8, 1895. Despite their bushy tails and similar name, Maine coons do not come from crossing a cat with a raccoon. That's just a myth. But most do like playing fetch and some communicate with birdlike chirps.

SELKIRK REX

HOMELAND Wyoming, U.S.A.

IDENTIFYING FEATURES A supersoft, full coat so curly that this cat looks as if it's had a perm

FUN TO KNOW The Selkirk's curly hair appeared naturally in a calico kitten born in 1987 in an animal shelter. A Wyoming breeder mated this cat with a prize-winning Persian, and a new breed was born. She named it "Selkirk", in honour of her stepfather. Besides their curly hair, which can come in any colour, Selkirks also have curly whiskers!

ABYSSINIAN

HOMELAND Unknown

IDENTIFYING FEATURES Green or gold, almond-shaped eyes and a special kind of tabby coat

FUN TO KNOW Abyssinians, or Abys, are an old breed. They got their name because the first ones exhibited in American cat shows came from the African country of Ethiopia, formerly known as Abyssinia. Athletic and lively, most Abys dislike being held. But they're very smart. When author Sheila Burnford wanted a companion for Simon, the Siamese cat in *The Incredible Journey,* she chose an Abyssinian.

PERSIAN

HOMELAND Iran (formerly Persia)

IDENTIFYING FEATURES A broad, flat face with a smushed-in nose and a luxurious, long coat

FUN TO KNOW Persians are the most popular cat breed. They make up three-quarters of all registered purebred cats and sometimes appear in movies. A white Persian named Snowbell starred in *Stuart Little,* and even threatened to eat the mouse. Owners love stroking Persians' long, silky coats, but the cats need daily brushing to prevent matting. The breed suffers from breathing problems due to their abnormally flat noses.

SIAMESE

HOMELAND
Thailand
(formerly Siam)

IDENTIFYING
FEATURES Long,
slender body
with a wedge-
shaped head, blue eyes, and big
ears. Recognized by dark coloured
"points"—on the face, ears, legs, and
tail—against a lighter coloured body.

FUN TO KNOW Named for their country
of origin, Siamese cats were unknown
outside of Asia until the 19th century.
Rutherford B. Hayes (U.S. president
from 1877 to 1881) owned the first
one ever brought to America. Named
Siam, she was a favourite of the
president's 12-year-old daughter,
Fanny. Most Siamese cats "talk"
constantly and dislike being left alone.

SPHYNX

HOMELAND
Toronto, Canada

IDENTIFYING
FEATURES
Warm to the
touch and
nearly bald, with
wrinkled skin and a long rat tail

FUN TO KNOW Most Sphynx cats are
loving and affectionate and get
along well with dogs. But if you are
allergic to cats, getting a Sphynx
won't help. That's because fur
doesn't cause allergies. The sniffling
comes from a chemical found in cat
saliva, which is left on a cat's fur and
skin during grooming. Also, Sphynx
cats often have problems of their
own. Their lack of fur makes them
vulnerable to sunburn in summer
and cold in winter.

RAGDOLL

HOMELAND
California,
U.S.A.

IDENTIFYING
FEATURES Gentle
giants, up to
three feet
(90 cm) long and weighing up to 35
pounds (15 kg), with silky, semi-long
hair and bright blue eyes

FUN TO KNOW Calm and relaxed,
ragdolls get their name from the fact
that they go completely limp when
held. Many of these cats act like big
puppies and follow their owners
from room to room. They're slow to
mature, taking as long as three to
four years to reach their adult size
and colour.

EXOTIC

HOMELAND
United States

IDENTIFYING
FEATURES
Identical to
Persians, except
for having a
shorter, denser coat

FUN TO KNOW Exotics are a new breed,
"invented" in 1967. With their cuddly
personalities and thick, plush coats,
they're like live teddy bears. Some
people call them the "lazy man's
Persian" because their shorter fur
doesn't mat or tangle as much. This
makes them easier to groom, although
they still need brushing twice a week.
Like Persians, Exotics sometimes
suffer from breathing problems.

MANX

HOMELAND The Isle of Man, off the coast of Great Britain

IDENTIFYING FEATURES They're missing a tail

FUN TO KNOW According to legend, the Manx was the last animal to board the Ark. Impatient to set sail, Noah slammed the door shut and accidentally cut off the cat's tail. The true story is that inbreeding of the island cats caused tailless kittens. Today, Manx cats are the symbol of the Isle of Man, where they appear on coins and postage stamps.

SAVANNAH

HOMELAND United States

IDENTIFYING FEATURES Recognized by their spotted coat and long legs, they look like wild leopards

FUN TO KNOW The Savannah is the largest domestic cat. It was created in 1986 by crossing a house cat with a serval—an African wild cat that hunts gazelles. Fear over what these big hunters could do if they got loose makes them illegal in some U.S. states. Hard to come by, they cost up to £27,000 apiece. The King of Morocco owns one.

EGYPTIAN MAU

HOMELAND Egypt

IDENTIFYING FEATURES Medium-size body with unusual green eyes and an evenly spotted coat

FUN TO KNOW "Mau" is Egyptian for "sacred cat". The distinctive markings on the Egyptian Mau look like those of cats painted on Egyptian tombs and scrolls over 2,000 years ago. Back then, killing a cat was punishable by death. The Egyptian queen Cleopatra painted her eyes to match those of her cat. And if a cat died, its owners shaved off their eyebrows in grief.

EVERYDAY CATS

HOMELAND Could be anywhere

IDENTIFYING FEATURES Found in all sizes, shapes, colours, and patterns

FUN TO KNOW More than 95 percent of the world's pet cats are nonpedigree. Moggies are born of parents that found each other. Humans had nothing to do with it. Everyday cats are hardy, adaptable, and easy to care for, and usually live longer than purebreds. You can find one at an animal shelter, or maybe one will find you. Everyday cats are clever that way.

Egyptian Mau

COAT OF MANY
COLOURS

Although domestic cats come in a dizzying array of colours, they all descend from the same tabby-patterned wildcat, a light brown feline with black stripes. Want proof? Just look at any cat in bright light to see faint stripes on their solid-coloured fur. Cat colours have changed over thousands of years. But a 2012 study revealed that our felines are still stereotyped based on ancient superstitions. Many people believe that orange cats are friendly, white cats are snobs, and tortoiseshell cats are easiest to train. And "unlucky" black cats? Many shelters still find these furry friends are tough to adopt out. Superstition aside, here's the truth about some common cat colours:

WHITE

White kitties look elegant, but they have a sad secret. The same gene that makes them white also leaves one of every five white cats deaf. Odds are worse for blue-eyed white cats, with three out of four inheriting deafness. So how do the white-furred, blue-eyed celebrity cats from cat food commercials manage? Not to worry. Most of them likely have top-notch hearing, since all are trained with clickers to perform on cue.

TORTOISESHELL

Tortoiseshell cats are a swirl of black, red, and maybe some white. They're almost always female, because cats carry colour genes on the X chromosome, and females have two of them. Males only have one X, plus a Y. So they can be red or black, but not both. (Any chromosome can carry no-colour white.) Eddie, a male tortoiseshell from England, is the rare exception. Only two or three male tortoiseshells are born there each year.

BLACK

Dark fur doesn't make a dark personality or bad luck. Take Sable, a large black cat from Richland, Washington, U.S.A., that is so trusted that he was awarded for his work as a safety patrol for students crossing the street. The only black cat owners prone to bad luck are those with severe allergies. Hospital researchers have found that black cats trigger allergies more than their colourful tabby relatives. Black cats pose no allergy problems outdoors, but indoors? *Fur*-geddaboutit!

CALICO

A calico cat is a tortoiseshell with clear-cut patches of white, usually on the face, belly, and legs. Perhaps the world's most famous calico cat was Scarlett, who bravely made five trips into a burning building in Brooklyn, New York, U.S.A., to save her kittens. Her eyes and face were severely burned during the rescue, but she and four of her kittens emerged safely and were adopted by loving families.

RED

What do Crookshanks from the Harry Potter movies and Garfield the comic cat have in common? They're red tabbies! They are commonly called ginger or marmalade. Tabbies can actually be any colour as long as they have faint dark stripes on their coats. These markings help tabbies blend in with brush and grass while stalking prey. Another way to spot a tabby is the "M" shape on their foreheads.

FUN and GAMES

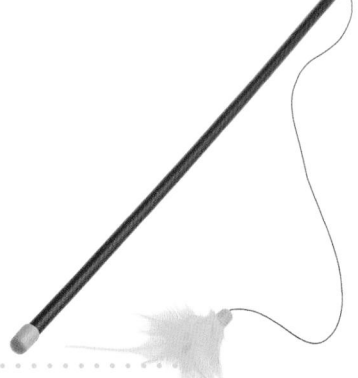

GO FISH

Remember, cats like toys that fall apart. So forget the pet store. Make your own fishing rod toy out of stuff you have lying around the house. If your cat tears it apart in a pretend hunt, great! But don't let him eat the lure! Cats love to eat string and thread and can get very sick. When one toy dies, make him another. Here's how:

1. Tie a string, about as long as your arm, on the end of a skinny stick.

2. Wrap sticky tape around the tip of the stick to hold the string in place.

3. Tie a "lure" on the string. This could be a feather, a small ball of aluminium foil, or short pieces of ribbon.

4. Now think and act like a mouse.

5. Snatch the lure quickly away from your cat, not toward her, as if you're running away.

6. Let her catch you.

7. Escape again and hide under a bookcase or behind a chair. Scoot out quickly or sneak across the floor. Vary your speed.

8. Let her catch you again.

9. Now wave your rod and "fly" like a bird, but stay within reach.

10. Three catches , and she's out. Reward her with a yummy treat.

Domestic longhair (Brown tabby)

POOF AND POP

You can now buy catnip bubbles, which are irresistible to kitties, and can be bought in most pet shops. Using the wand provided with the bottle, blow bubbles at your cat. Watch him bat and chase them. Remember to give him a treat at the end.

PUZZLE PLAY

Want a fit, healthy cat? Make him work for his supper. That's what keepers do for big cats in the zoo. Searching for food exercises their brains as well as their bodies and keeps them from being bored.

1. Find an empty plastic bottle.

2. Cut large holes in the sides.

3. Put a little dry cat food in the bottle. (Measure the amount and deduct it from your kitty's supper. Otherwise, he might get fat.)

4. Screw on the cap, and let your cat paw out the food.

5. Once he figures it out, make another feeder with smaller holes.

BAGS AND BOXES

1. Put a Ping Pong ball inside an empty tissue box for your cat to bat around.

2. Make a comfy cat bed. Remove the lid from a cardboard box. Cut down one side so she can enter easily. Use a blanket scrap for a mattress.

3. Cut the bottoms out of several paper bags. Tape them end to end to make a tunnel. Set the tunnel on the floor, place a treat inside, and watch your kitty scoot through it.

4. Put a catnip mouse inside an open paper bag. Lay the bag on the floor, and watch your cat go into a trance. (Catnip is safe and nonaddictive, but not all cats react to it.)

PaWS, LOOK, & LiSTEN QUiZ

CATS AREN'T ALWAYS VERY TALKATIVE, so it's up to us to pay attention when they do "speak". Take this quiz to discover how careful listening can keep you safe.

1. Kids are most often bitten by

- A. Frightened cats
- B. Strays
- C. Hungry cats
- D. Persian cats

2. Cats sometimes bite when they

- A. Are playing rough
- B. No longer want to be stroked
- C. Lack an escape route
- D. All of the above

3. If a cat rolls over exposing his belly, you should

- A. Rub his stomach
- B. Look, but don't touch
- C. Poke him with a stick
- D. Tickle his feet

4. What's your best defense if a cat grabs your arm and bites your wrist?

- A. Yell for help
- B. Shake your arm hard
- C. Make your arm and hand go limp
- D. Stomp your feet

Answers to Stay Safe Around Cats

1. A. Frightened cats would almost always rather run away than fight. But all cats, even cuddly lap sitters, use their claws in self-defense. So beware any feline that feels it is cornered and can't escape.

2. D. Pain, fear, stroking, and rough play all can cause cats to attack. Protect yourself by staying away from any cat with flattened ears, a twitching tail, and a hunched body.

3. B. When a cat turns belly-up, he wants attention. But he is not asking to be poked, stroked, or tickled. Rub his belly, and he may grab your hand and rake it with his claws.

4. C. If you're stroking a cat, and he bites you, he wants you to quit. So stop moving your hand and let your arm go limp. That will reassure him, and he'll let go.

5. When encountering a strange cat, you should

- **A.** Ignore him until he comes to you
- **B.** Pick him up immediately
- **C.** Pet him on his back using long strokes
- **D.** Chase him until you catch him

6. Never disturb a cat that is

- **A.** Sleeping
- **B.** Hissing
- **C.** Miaowing
- **D.** Washing her face

7. A hard stare, lowered head, and puffy tail are all signs of

- **A.** A hungry cat
- **B.** A playful cat
- **C.** An anxious cat
- **D.** An angry cat

8. What's the best sign that a cat is friendly?

- **A.** Body rubbing
- **B.** Pricked ears
- **C.** A wagging tail
- **D.** Half-closed eyes

British longhair

5. A. How friendly a cat is depends on how many people he met and how much handling he received as a kitten. Never force yourself on a strange cat. Always let him make the first move.

6. B. It's fine to approach a cat that is sleeping, miaowing, or grooming. She's feeling comfortable and relaxed. Not so a hissing cat. That hiss is a warning meant to scare you away.

7. D. An angry cat is an aggressive cat. Rather than trying to flee, an angry cat leans forward and prepares to attack. He might even growl. But if you back off, so will he.

8. A. Pricked ears, half-closed eyes, and a wagging tail all have multiple meanings. But body rubbing is easy to interpret. Why? Because it involves the whole cat. Never judge a cat by one body part alone.

ReSOURCES

Pros Who Can Help

Blue Cross for Pets
Blue Cross for Pets offers treatment and re-homing services for a variety of pets every year. They also provide education and workshops to promote the importance of being a responsible pet owner.

» www.bluecross.org.uk

Cat Action Trust
The Cat Action Trust works to improve the welfare of feral cats. Feral cat colonies have been killed in the past as they were deemed to be pests. The Cat Action Trust fights to save these cats by trapping, neutering and returning them to their colonies, ensuring a more humane way of controlling their numbers.

» www.catactiontrust.org.uk

Cats Protection
Cats Protection has become one of the UK's leading feline welfare organizations. It helps re-home thousands of cats each year via its adoption centres. It also provides owners with advice on how to care for their feline friends.

» www.cats.org.uk

Cruelty Free International
This international organization campaigns against experimenting on animals all over the world. It investigates and challenges organizations that use animal testing, and promotes alternative methods.

» www.crueltyfreeinternational.org

Royal Society for the Prevention of Cruelty to Animals (RSPCA)
This is the UK's largest animal welfare charity. Under the "Advice and Welfare" tab, you'll find great cat care tips. You can also click on "Ask a question" and ask experts at the RSPCA questions about cat welfare.

» www.rspca.org.uk

Scottish Society for the Prevention of Cruelty to Animals (Scottish SPCA)
The Scottish SPCA is Scotland's animal welfare charity—it has been helping animals in Scotland for over 175 years. They organize events, raising money to help educate children to look after their pets well, as well as helping re-home thousands of animals each year.

» www.scottishspca.org

Wood Green, The Animals Charity
Wood Green, The Animals Charity cares for and re-homes all types of animals. Under the "Pet advice" tab, there is plenty of information about how to care for kitties—from what to do if you lose your cat to the importance of vaccinating your pet.

» www.woodgreen.org.uk

On Screen and In Print

BOOKS

National Geographic Readers: Cats vs. Dogs (Level 3)
Elizabeth Carney
National Geographic Children's Books, 2011

Everything Big Cats
Elizabeth Carney
National Geographic Children's Books, 2011

Everything Pets
James Spears With Virginia Morell
National Geographic Children's Books, 2013

Why Is My Cat Doing That?
Sarah Heath
Thunder Bay Press, 2009

MOVIES

Extraordinary Cats
Nature, PBS, 1999

Science of Cats DVD
National Geographic, 2010

The Secret Life of Cats DVD
National Geographic, 2010

WEBSITES

Animal Planet
www.animalplanet.com/tv-shows/cats-101

BBC NEWS Science and Environment
"Secret Life of the Cat: What Do Our Feline Companions Get Up To?"
bbc.com/news/science-environment-22567526. Click on a particular cat and see its route around the neighbourhood, as tracked by GPS and kitty cams

National Geographic
"Domestic Cat"
animals.nationalgeographic.com/animals/mammals/domestic-cat/

"My Shot: Cats"
kids-myshot.nationalgeographic.com/search?s=cats&t=photo&submit

"Wild Side of Cats"
channel.nationalgeographic.com/wild/galleries/wild-side-of-cats/#wide-eyed2-1005417

"Can You Really Train Your Cat?"
video.nationalgeographic.com/video/news/training-circus-cats-vin

INDeX

Published by Collins
An imprint of HarperCollins Publishers
Westerhill Road
Bishopbriggs
Glasgow G64 2QT
www.harpercollins.co.uk

In association with National Geographic
Partners, LLC

NATIONAL GEOGRAPHIC and the Yellow Border
Design are trademarks of the National
Geographic Society, used under license.

First published 2015

ISBN 9780008257903

10 9 8 7 6 5 4 3 2 1

Printed in China

If you would like to comment on any aspect of
this book, please contact us at the above
address or online.
natgeokidsbooks.co.uk
collins.reference@harpercollins.co.uk

Paper from responsible sources.